THE JOY OF ORTHODOXY

ORTHODOX LOGOS PUBLISHING

THE JOY OF ORTHODOXY

by Deacon David Lochbihler, J.D.

Front cover photograph by Callie Rae Kyhl

Back cover photograph by Micah Marie Friedrich

Book cover design and interior layout by Max Mendor

Publishers Maxim Hodak & Max Mendor

© 2022, Deacon David Lochbihler, J.D.

© 2022, Orthodox Logos Publishing,

The Netherlands

www.orthodoxlogos.com

ISBN: 978-1-80484-003-0

This book is in copyright. No part of this publication may be reproduced, stored in a retrieval system or transmitted in any form or by any means without the prior permission in writing of the publisher, nor be otherwise circulated in any form of binding or cover other than that in which it is published without a similar condition, including this condition, being imposed on the subsequent purchaser.

DEACON DAVID LOCHBIHLER, J.D.

THE JOY OF ORTHODOXY

ORTHODOX LOGOS PUBLISHING

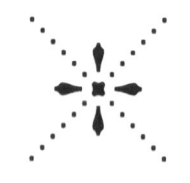

CONTENTS

ACKNOWLEDGEMENTS 11

PROLOGUE: WONDER 15

CHAPTER ONE – MONDAY:
THE VIRTUE OF HUMILITY 25

CHAPTER TWO – TUESDAY:
THE VIRTUE OF PURITY 36

CHAPTER THREE – WEDNESDAY:
THE VIRTUE OF HOLINESS 50

CHAPTER FOUR – THURSDAY:
THE VIRTUE OF LOVE 66

CHAPTER FIVE – FRIDAY:
THE VIRTUE OF LONGSUFFERING 81

CHAPTER SIX – SATURDAY:
THE VIRTUE OF PRAYER 88

CHAPTER SEVEN – SUNDAY:
THE VIRTUE OF JOY 104

EPILOGUE: LIVING THE VIRTUOUS LIFE EACH DAY . . . 124

BIBLIOGRAPHY 134

ABOUT THE AUTHOR 141

To Luci Marie

<u>The Days of the Week</u>
The bunnies hop on Monday.
Children run on Tuesday.
Flowers bloom on Wednesday.
Walk your dog on Thursday.
Play games on Friday.
Eat treats on Saturday.
And everyone rests on Holy Sunday.
Millie Ruth Frazier, *Poems All Year Round*

ACKNOWLEDGEMENTS

Most all of the research and scholarship in this book was learned at the Antiochian Village in Pennsylvania through the Saint Stephen's Course of Studies and Master's Degree Program in Applied Orthodox Theology. Although there are thousands of Orthodox books in libraries, seminaries, and bookstores, I tried to make this book unique in two ways. First, I wanted to focus primarily on the pure joy inherent in being or becoming Orthodox. Second, I tried to combine personal stories, scholarly work, and practical advice in one manuscript. I hope *The Joy of Orthodoxy* touches you, my beloved reader, in at least one of these two avenues of emphasis. Orthodox Joy helps us stand strong during these historically challenging times.

I want to begin by thanking Metropolitan Joseph of the Antiochian Archdiocese of North America for approving my ordination to the diaconate at the Western Rite Conference in Fort Worth, Texas, Bishop John for ordaining me at Saint Patrick Orthodox Church on Saint Patrick's Day 17 March 2019, and Bishop Thomas for his deep love for and faithful friendship with our dear parishioners in the pews of Saint Patrick Orthodox Church. The wonder-filled people of Saint Patrick are supreme. Receiving innumerable letters from pen pals Maggie McLaurin,

Luci Marie, Evangeline Sophia, Leah Lanelle, Olivia Anne, James Patrick, Sola Elise, Millie Ruth, the Charismatic Kyhls, the Fantastic Friedrichs, the Mighty Meadors, the dynamic Dohms, the Wondrous Wetzels, and the Faithful Fraziers brings great joy to my heart. These wonder-filled Saint Patrick families and friends epitomize the essence of Orthodox Joy.

Special thanks to David and Jo Thoburn and my students, parents, and colleagues at The Fairfax Christian School in Dulles, Virginia, where I teach fourth grade. I also am extremely grateful to Metropolitan Kallistos Ware, Father Anthony Messeh, Father Peter Gillquist of blessed memory, Father Alexander Atty of blessed memory, Father Patrick Cardine, and Father Thomas Palke for guiding me into Orthodoxy.

I completed the first draft of this book at Our Lady and Saint Laurence Monastery in the Rocky Mountains of Colorado. A heartfelt thank you to Dom Theodore, Brother Joseph, Dame Sophia of blessed memory, Dame Olga of blessed memory, and Marcão for making me feel so at home during my summer travels. Summer vacation also is a great time to visit and serve with Father Peter Jon Gillquist and his mother Khouria Marilyn of All Saints Orthodox Church in Bloomington, Indiana.

Growing up in the 1960's in Fort Wayne, Indiana, it was a joy to live only two blocks from Saint Charles Borromeo Church and School at our spacious home with the big backyard on Elwood Drive. Grandpa Vincent William and Grandma Mamie Lucy of blessed memory, Dad Frederick Louis of blessed memory, and Mom Marion Helen, siblings Fred, Lyn, and Vince, and cats Angel Face and Dusty, built a marvelous life together with an abundance of joyful memories. Grandpa immigrated into the United States from Lithuania in 1888 at the age of eighteen with two cents in his pocket. Not knowing any English, he learned the language and became an accomplished Chicago attorney. Grandma lived to be 103 and loved praying the Rosary twice daily. Mom and Dad met at Marshall Field's in downtown Chicago after World War Two, with Dad serving in Guadalcanal and earning the rank of Colonel in the United States Army. Mom's drive and Dad's calm were the perfect combination to raise four successful children.

After getting married on New Year's Eve in 1948, Mom and Dad's first pet was a boxer named Putch Pye. Mom and Dad built three houses: the Frank Lloyd Wright house at Ogden Dunes, the Graham Woods house near Chesterton, and our most memorable childhood home at Elwood Drive in Fort Wayne. We moved to Penrose Drive during my four years at Bishop Dwenger High School and adopted a remarkable white American Eskimo dog named Shell-a-Babe, although we kids called her Pupface. Mom recently celebrated her one hundredth birthday with her beloved family, living a century while successfully schooling us for many years with her superior skill as our family's finest reigning Gin Rummy Hall of Fame Champion. My older siblings Fred, Lyn, and Vince are my lifelong best friends. Additional sources of joy are those marrying into our family, Darlene of blessed memory, Judy, Whitney, Kevin, and Tania, as well as my nieces and nephews Angela Marie, Stephanie Lynn, Brett Jordan, and Frederick Lochbihler IV, and grandnephews Grant, Nolan, Isaac, and our newest additions to our small clan, Frederick Fuechee Lochbihler V and his new baby sister Leilana. I love and thank my amazing family.

This work would not be worthy to print without the expert advice of Father James Hamrick and the editing assistance of Brian Donohue and Scott Richardson. Finally, a heartfelt thank you to publishers Maxim Hodak and Max Mendor of Orthodox Logos in the Nederland for publishing this book. Your kindness and patience (long-suffering) are deeply appreciated.

I finish this manuscript, a project begun many years ago, and forward it to the Netherlands from my favourite childhood vacation venue, McCormick's Creek State Park in Indiana, after celebrating Mom's 100th birthday and spending precious summer travel time with my family. I would love to hear from you, my beloved reader, if any small part of this work touches your heart.

> Friends in Jesus and Mary,
> Deacon David Lochbihler, J.D.
> Saint Patrick Orthodox Church
> Sunday 7 August 2022
> Canyon Inn, McCormick's Creek State Park, Indiana
> orthodoxdeacondavid@gmail.com

PROLOGUE

WONDER

A child's heart is filled with wonder, and from wonder springs forth poetry. "Because Jesus' heart is a poetic one, one who follows him sees rightly with his heart, a heart that in devotion seeks to die for that which it loves."[1] The poet understands and appreciates the mystery of wonder.

William Wordsworth clearly articulates the interplay between our childlike wonder and our adult faith:

> The Child is father of the Man;
> And I could wish my days to be
> Bound each to each by natural piety.[2]

Gerard Manley Hopkins sees the beauty of wonder clearly and can say, "The world is charged with the grandeur of God."[3] The Paschal Mystery, in which we know the Friday

---

[1] Metropolitan Philip Saliba and Joseph Allen, *Meeting the Incarnate God* (Brookline, MA: Holy Cross Orthodox Press, 2008), 49.

[2] William Wordsworth, " 'My Heart Leaps Up When I Behold,' "*Selected Poems of William Wordsworth*, ed. Solomon Francis Gingerich (Boston: Houghton Mifflin Company, 1923), 66.

[3] Gerard Manley Hopkins, "God's Grandeur," *Poems of Gerard*

of Jesus' death will be forever "Good," is profound and requires a child's heart filled with wonder in order to appreciate fully its significance. We can meet our God made Incarnate to the extent our hearts look deeply at life with the eyes of both a child and a poet.

"Truly I say to you, unless you are converted and become like children, you shall not enter the kingdom of heaven."[4] To be a child of God means to see again with the inner eyes of faith, to truly wonder. A child is devoted to his or her best friends Jesus and Mary with a pure heart and the experience of joyful humility. Baptized as infants the month after we were born, our entire lives are sacramental and filled with mystery.

My own childhood was filled with wonder. As the youngest of four in a devout Roman Catholic family, my sacramental life began early, with Confession in second grade, Communion in third, and Confirmation in fourth. We would play "Priest" as children. I remember wearing a red towel tied to my neck and draped down my back, looking more like Superman than a priest. We pretended with childlike sincerity to baptize our cat Angel Face with water. For Communion, we would use a hot iron and Wonder Bread wrapped in tin foil to make little communion wafers. I think back to my own wonder-filled childhood and the devotion I experienced so personally and deeply as I walked to weekday morning Mass during the summer between third and fourth grades, loving Je-

---

Manley Hopkins, ed. W. H. Gardner (New York: Oxford University Press, 1948), 70.

[4] Matthew 18:3 NASB.

sus and Mary as intimate friends, looking with awe at the giant crucifix above the altar, and first nurturing in my heart the desire to become a priest. The holiness and joy of church life touched the deepest part of our young and enthusiastic hearts.

My life has been filled with joy, but it only has been upon my coming home and becoming Orthodox that my "joy may be complete."[5] I was so blessed to experience Chrismation into the Holy Orthodox Church on the most special Feast of the Nativity of the Blessed Virgin Mary. Serving at the Divine Liturgy as a Deacon during our Sunday morning Mass continually brings this fervent devotion to Jesus and Mary back to the forefront of my heart, and with childlike faith and devotion I rejoice each Mass to meet the Incarnate God at both the Holy Altar and in the deepest recesses of my heart.

The Incarnation of Jesus Christ changed everything and serves as the epicenter of human history. "In the beginning was the Word, and the Word was with God, and the Word was God."[6] Before the Incarnation, humanity found itself enslaved to sin, sickness, and death. After the Incarnation, God the Son descended from heaven and became human, both sanctifying us and all of creation like never before while offering us the opportunity to be free from sin and able to enjoy eternal life with God.

On an infinitely smaller yet quite personal level, becoming Orthodox changes everything. You discover a

---

[5] John 16:24 NRSV.
[6] John 1:1 NASB.

new world seen anew with the childlike eyes of wonder. Humility is the way you want to live. Purity becomes second nature. Holiness becomes the most important clarion call to your soul. Love becomes God's primary mission for you. Longsuffering in your life merges with the Cross and Passion of Jesus. Prayer becomes someone you are rather than something you do. This embrace of childlike wonder culminates on Sunday as you live first and foremost to experience the joy of receiving the Body and Blood of Christ in the Eucharist, the highlight and culmination of each and every week.

"Rejoice always; pray without ceasing; in everything give thanks; for this is God's will for you in Christ Jesus."[7] Joy, Prayer, Thanksgiving: these three virtues as much as any permeate our journey within the Orthodox Church. Our heart's response described by Saint Paul becomes a daily reality: we rejoice not occasionally but always; we pray not just on Sunday but without ceasing; our hearts overflow with gratitude. Our best friends Jesus the Christ and Mary the Theotokos reside deep down inside our hearts and guide our thoughts, words, and deeds every minute of every day.

Becoming Orthodox opens one's world to wonder like never before. "And now here is my secret, a very simple secret: It is only with the heart that one can see rightly; what is essential is invisible to the eye."[8] With these words, Antoine de Saint-Exupéry describes the essence of seeing

---

[7] 1 Thessalonians 5:16-18 NASB.

[8] Antoine de Saint-Exupéry, *The Little Prince* (San Diego: Harcourt Brace, 1971), 73.

our world through the inner eyes of faith. This ongoing quest for the essential and the invisible best expresses my lifelong journey into Orthodoxy.

The year is 1976, and I am a sophomore at the University of Notre Dame. Enrolled in a course entitled "Introduction to Philosophy," I expected to be challenged with the philosophical discourses of Descartes and Hume. Instead, Professor Joe Evans began our collegiate initiation into Philosophy with the classic children's tale *The Little Prince* by Antoine de Saint-Exupéry. It was then I learned the Secret of the Fox, "that it is only with the heart that one can see rightly; what is essential is invisible to the eye."[9] Fast forward thirty-six years later as His Eminence Metropolitan Kallistos Ware speaks about how to incorporate the Jesus Prayer into our daily lives at Saint Mark Coptic Orthodox Church in Fairfax, Virginia, on Saturday evening 23 June 2012. He also quoted the Secret of the Fox from *The Little Prince* and later sent to me a postcard from Oxford in Great Britain to reaffirm, "The book is a great favourite of mine."[10] Citing the Secret of the Fox, Metropolitan Ware invited us to pray the Jesus Prayer for fifteen minutes each day and then spend the rest of the day loving others with Christ's love.

My long journey into Orthodoxy took many unexpected twists and turns anchored with one great constant: the Secret of the Fox. My life has been a gradual learning of this special secret, a shift from the head to the heart, a

---

[9] Ibid.
[10] Kallistos Ware, Letter to David Lochbihler, 28 July 2012.

deeper appreciation of the invisible, a journey with much joy along the narrow path towards the Way, the Truth, and the Life. The complex simplicity of my lifelong journey into Orthodoxy frequently surprises me with newfound wonder.

In my own odyssey into Orthodoxy, although books took me some distance towards the truth, the Divine Liturgy has been by far the best teacher. In this regard, the Divine Liturgy emphasizes the great mysteries from the Annunciation to Pentecost surrounding the manifestation of Jesus Christ our Saviour. "O God the Great and the Eternal, Who formed man in incorruption, and death which entered into the world by the envy of the devil, You have destroyed, by the lifegiving manifestation of Your Only-Begotten Son, our Lord, God and Saviour Jesus Christ."[11]

The Divine Liturgy is an indescribably magnificent feast. "Feast means *joy*."[12] The Divine Liturgy experienced as "heaven on earth"[13] best exemplifies this unbounded joy and serves as the most constant anchor of our lives. "Our Church remains a liturgical Church *par excellence* not only in the sense of the uninterruptedness of her ancient tradition of worship, but also because of the place which worship occupies in the life of the faithful, because of the

---

[11] *The Coptic Liturgy of St. Basil* (Cairo, Egypt: St. John the Beloved Publishing House, 1993), 216.

[12] Alexander Schmemann, *For the Life of the World*, 2nd ed. rev. (Crestwood, NY: St. Vladimir's Seminary Press, 1973), 63 (emphasis in original).

[13] Ibid., 30.

special love the faithful have for the church building and its services."[14]

We experience the pinnacle of Orthodox wonder during the celebration of the Divine Liturgy. Notre Dame Professor of Philosophy Joe Evans used to tell us, "No wonder, no philosophy… and no wonder!" Wonder erupts anew during the Divine Liturgy. As we kneel during the Western Rite Canon at Saint Patrick Orthodox Church, as the priest boldly declares in the words of Christ, "This is My Body; This is My Blood," we witness with our own eyes the greatest miracle we could neither seek nor imagine on our own initiative. Minutes later during the Divine Liturgy, when we eat the Body of Christ and drink His Blood, we live totally and completely in communion with Christ. "He that eateth my flesh, and drinketh my blood, dwelleth in me, and I in him."[15]

"The sting of death is sin, and the power of sin is the law; but thanks be to God, who gives us the victory through our Lord Jesus Christ."[16] How soon we forget this heavenly victory. Before we leave the church parking lot, our minds already shift from the inner joy and peace immersed within our Divine Liturgy to the mundane activities of the day and the upcoming workweek. The Eucharistic miracle recedes in our minds; the joyful wonder touching our hearts is fleeting. How can we carry this joyful wonder with us into our homes and jobs? How

---

[14] Alexander Schmemann, *Introduction to Liturgical Theology* (Crestwood, NY: St. Vladimir's Seminary Press, 2003), 27.
[15] John 6:56 KJV.
[16] 1 Corinthians 15:56-57 NASB.

can we bring this joyful wonder to the forefront of our everyday lives, every minute of every day?

The answer to these twin questions lies in Saint Paul's simple command: "Rejoice always; pray without ceasing; in everything give thanks; for this is God's will for you in Christ Jesus."[17] With joyful hearts both immersed in prayer and filled with thanksgiving, we embrace Orthodoxy with a conscious decision to seek God continually by living a virtuous life, every minute of every day.

This book provides a practical way forward by inviting you to focus your attention on seven critical virtues, one for every day of the week. Although the Resurrection of Jesus on Sunday is the most important day of the week, I write this book beginning with the drudgery of Monday as many of us commute to work to begin a challenging, worldly workweek. We labor anew each Monday morning with our eyes fixed on the *telos* of next Sunday morning's Divine Liturgy.

As you go to bed on Sunday night, you celebrate the Resurrection Joy and prepare for your workweek with Joyful Humility. The Virtue of Humility greets your heart as you awaken the next morning to get ready for work. You repeat this cycle as you go to sleep each night and arise in the morning, focusing your heart on each day's unique virtue. You take some time to meditate on these respective realities throughout the day, concentrating on a different virtue each day of the week. Here are the seven focal points for this ongoing daily adventure:

---

[17] 1 Thessalonians 5:16-18 NASB.

Monday: HUMILITY
Tuesday: PURITY
Wednesday: HOLINESS
Thursday: LOVE
Friday: LONGSUFFERING
Saturday: PRAYER
Sunday: JOY

This book offers a very simple strategy to strive towards unceasing prayer. As you begin your workweek, you decide on Sunday night to exemplify the Virtue of Humility on Monday. At home you place the needs and hopes of your family before your own, and at work you put your boss and your co-workers first. On Tuesday, you shift your focus to the Virtue of Purity, to dwell upon what it really means to embrace a pure lifestyle. Because "the pure in heart… shall see God,"[18] you make purity your primary goal this day. You seek each Wednesday during the day to look for ways to exemplify the Virtue of Holiness. At lunch and during a coffee break, you close your physical eyes for a brief minute to ponder with the inner eyes of faith the unseen holiness of God all around you. You begin each Thursday looking for opportunities to love God by both loving your neighbor and forgiving your enemies. You fulfill the Virtue of Love by actually trying to listen and learn rather than judge and command. Amidst your hurried Friday and the happy end of the long workweek, with the start of the weekend only hours away, you di-

---

[18] Matthew 5:8 NKJV.

rect your heart to the Passion of Christ and rejoice with the Virtue of Longsuffering at the thought of how His ultimate sacrifice made all things new. This is the perfect day, throughout the day, to keep your gaze fixed upon the Cross of the Crucified Christ. Saturday with your family at home, you renew your commitment to God by seeking the solace and silence inherent in the Virtue of Prayer. Finally on Sunday with your spiritual family at church, you wonder at the Real Presence of Christ in the Eucharist, the Eucharist as the sacrament of thanksgiving, and keep the morning's reception of Holy Communion fresh in your mind and heart all day long. Indeed, you strive to keep the Virtue of Joy at the forefront of your heart not only during this most holy day of the Resurrection, all day, but also during the workweek until next Sunday's Holy Communion.

By focusing on these seven virtues, with the emphasis on a different theme every day, and concentrating on that single virtue throughout any given day, "we are taking every thought captive to the obedience of Christ."[19] This book provides a simple day-by-day strategy to deepen your communion with Christ while embracing a more virtuous life.

---

[19] 2 Corinthians 10:5b NASB.

CHAPTER ONE

MONDAY

THE VIRTUE OF HUMILITY

Don't be jealous or proud, but be humble and consider
others more important than yourselves
(Philippians 2:3 CEV).

Because humility is the entry or starting point for launching all the other virtues, we begin our Monday workweek pondering the Virtue of Humility.

I was blessed as a child to attend a neighborhood Roman Catholic Church with an excellent grade school, both church and school within walking distance from our house. We lived on Elwood Drive in Fort Wayne, Indiana, immersed in backyard baseball and football and neighborhood basketball. Emulating our heroes, we played Vida Blue Baseball, Lem Barney Football, and Rick Mount Basketball. Saint Charles Borromeo Catholic Church and School stood a mere two blocks away, and it became the center of our little childhood universe.

During the memorable summer between third and fourth grades, I remember walking the two blocks to go to morning Mass. One sad morning, on our front porch, Angel Face our beloved cat lay on her side, bleeding and dead. We never knew what happened, and we thought Angel Face, either after a catfight or a car, dragged herself home and died on our front porch. I remember walking to Mass the morning Angel Face died; going to church always seemed to make terrible things better.

My greatest childhood disappointment occurred during my eighth-grade school year. The great State of Indiana was and is the home of basketball, and my hero was Rick Mount, one of the best pure shooters in basketball. Rick played college ball at Purdue and later joined the Indiana Pacers. While competing for a roster spot on the basketball team in eighth grade, I wrote the number "10" with a magic marker for my boyhood hero Rick Mount on my T-shirt. One of the coaches told us, anyone who can sink four of five free throws "has it made," and I like my boyhood hero had a pretty good shot. I had two chances, five free throws each round, and all I needed to do was sink four of five to make the team. My first try, I hit the first three free throws but then missed the next two. My second try, I missed the first two free throws before nailing the last three in a row. A respectable six of ten, pretty good for an eighth grader. It was the start of winter in Indiana, and I had come to practice without my winter coat. As I left the gym at the end of tryouts, one the coaches told me, "You know, if you make the team, you really need to bring your winter coat." I thought I had it made! The next day, the team roster was posted on a list hung in the hallway. I still remember just staring at the list for the longest time and not seeing my name. Being cut in eighth grade, not making the basketball team, was the biggest disappointment of my grade school years.

The year 1968 changed American history and touched our lives forever, breaking through our suburban safety in Fort Wayne. During my fifth-grade year, the United States found herself in political upheaval. Senator Eugene McCarthy ran against the war raging in a faraway place called Vietnam and captured the New Hampshire primary, and President Lyndon Baines Johnson decided not to run for a second term. Mom and Dad did their best to keep us safe and protected from the turmoil of these tumultuous times. It was only years later that I learned an assassin gunned down Dr. Martin Luther King in Memphis on Friday, 4 April 1968. Although Dad was a staunch Republican, my oldest brother Fred volunteered for the Democrats as a high school junior, and we kids loved the candidacy of Senator Robert Francis Kennedy. Nearly five short years earlier, while I was in first grade, our school principal, speaking sadly and softly from the school speaker system, asked us to stand and pray as we learned an assassin's bullets struck President John Fitzgerald Kennedy dead in Dallas before sending us home. Now just a few short years later, his charismatic younger brother sought the Presidency.

On Wednesday, 23 April 1968, Mom and Dad took us to see Senator Kennedy speak at Concordia Senior College. We sat in the very first row facing the stage, all the way to the left by the side aisle. Someone important, perhaps from the Senator's staff, came up to us and said, "If you kids are really good, the Senator will walk right by here and shake your hands," and we sat silently and supremely excited, waiting in eager anticipation for Senator Kennedy's walk to the stage. Sure enough, the wildly popular Senator affectionately known as Bobby walked right past us as promised, and we were among his many supporters surrounding him right where we waited as he turned the corner towards the stage. Bobby walked right near us, surrounded and slowed by the mob of his affectionate supporters, moving ever so slowly around our corner seats. He moved so slowly, I was able to shake his hand not once but two or three times, the massive crowd almost immobilizing the Senator as he turned the corner. From the morning press release Dad secured from a local reporter, we heard only a brief mention about the Vietnam War, the heart of Bobby's candidacy. His Fort Wayne speech focused primarily on the rising costs of higher education and how our nation's resources could best be used to face our challenges at home rather than going towards "the monetary demands being made by the war in Vietnam."[20] Faced with the rising costs of college and other domestic concerns, the candidate said "that is all the more reason to get on with the task of making a peace, so we can tend to our problems in the United States."[21]

....

[20] Robert F. Kennedy, "Excerpts from Remarks," Concordia Senior College, Fort Wayne, Indiana, 23 April 1968, 2.
[21] Ibid.

Little did we know that nearly three weeks earlier, Senator Kennedy faced a potentially angry crowd in Indianapolis a few short hours after the assassination of Dr. Martin Luther King, Jr. Bobby began his short, unplanned speech by telling the crowd he just learned Dr. King had been killed. Referring to his older brother John's assassination, Senator Kennedy's call for love and compassion rather than division and hatred calmed the crowd. Unlike many American cities that night, there was no riot in Indianapolis.

Sirhan Sirhan shot Senator Robert Francis Kennedy on Wednesday, 5 June 1968, after the crucial California primary. Eleven years old at the time, I awakened that fateful morning to overhear a radio account of the brutal assassination attempt. RFK died the next day, his untimely death spreading sadness throughout the summer of 1968 between my fifth- and sixth-grade years.

Seventh grade was my finest year in grade school forming friendships with Jeff, Kenny, and Tim as we focused on sports and science in the joyful classroom of Mrs. Theodora Schick of blessed memory. My personal childhood disappointment came one year later after I lost my dream to play for the Saint Charles Cardinal basketball team during my eighth-grade year. Humility springs from both the deep disappointments and inevitable sufferings we all experience. Yet we also may learn humility in success. Many of us soon realize that whether we achieve or endure, apart from Jesus we can accomplish absolutely nothing of lasting value and worth. "I am the vine, ye are the branches: He that abideth in me, and I in him, the same bringeth forth much fruit: for without me ye can do nothing."[22]

Humility needs to take root in the human heart. Abba Pior, a protégé of Abba Antony the Great, sat silently when a brother's sin was exposed. He left and later returned with a large sack filled with sand carried on his shoulder. He also carried a little sand in a bag ahead of him. " 'In this sack which contains much sand, are my sins which are many; I have put them behind me so as not to be troubled about them and so as not to weep; and see here are the little sins of my brother which are in front of me and I spend my time judging them. This is not right, I ought rather to carry my sins in front of me and concern myself with them, begging God to forgive me for them.' The Fathers stood up and said, 'Truly, this is the way of salvation.'"[23]

"The word 'humility' comes from the Latin word '*humus*' which means fertile ground."[24] Father Alexander Eichaninov writes, "Pride, self-esteem, vanity, to which we may add haughtiness, arrogance, conceit – all these are various aspects of one basic phenomenon: *concentration on self*."[25] As our sinful pride tends towards an overwhelming "concentration on self," only a humble heart

---

[22] John 15:5 KJV.

[23] *The Sayings of the Desert Fathers*, translated by Benedicta Ward (Kalamazoo, MI: Cistercian Publications, 1984), 199-200.

[24] Metropolitan Anthony Bloom, *Beginning to Pray* (New York: Paulist Press, 1982), 35.

[25] Alexander Eichaninov, *The Diary of a Russian Priest* (Crestwood, NY: St. Vladimir's Seminary Press, 1967), 247 (emphasis in original).

becomes a fertile ground for prayer and communion with God. Jesus takes root when planted in this fertile soil of humility so that, like Saint John the Baptist, we may begin to pray, "He must increase, but I must decrease."[26] Both Orthodox clergy and laity must strive to emulate the humility of Christ.

This perfect humility is personified in the "Word made flesh,"[27] Jesus dwelling in our midst. "The Church's ministry rests upon Christ's very person and being as the Son of God who became flesh in history."[28] Jesus' humble service as Good Shepherd expressed itself in seeking to fulfill God the Father's holy will by becoming the perfect prophet, king, and priest. The priest is called to present Christ to his flock, and both priest and people strive to live the words and actions of Jesus Christ. We don't just continue His earthly ministry; rather, He lives in and through our ministry and is the source of all we preach and do. Christ is especially present in the Eucharist, and His power and presence permeates all aspects of our lives as ministers.

Both the specific ministry of the clergy and the general ministry of the laity call us through the power of the Holy Spirit to humble service in the Church. For the apostles and disciples in their ministry as shepherds, three characteristics are required. First, the minister must be a man of God with words and deeds consistent with the virtues

---

[26] John 3:30 NASB.
[27] John 1:14 NKJV.
[28] Joseph J. Allen, *The Ministry of the Church* (Crestwood, NY: St. Vladimir's Seminary Press, 1968), 25.

"in conduct, in love, in spirit, in faith, in purity."[29] Indeed, "his entire life is to be aimed, not toward anything else in the world, but only toward God."[30] Second, the minister is to be both "the salt of the earth" and "the light of the world."[31] While salt both preserves and enlivens food, light reveals the truth embodied in Jesus "the light of the world."[32] Finally, the minister is called to suffer with others as good soldiers in the name of Christ. We are to embody the Crucified Christ and freely with courage and love enter into and be willing to share the painful suffering of our brothers and sisters. All are called to serve: the laity through their Baptism, the clergy through their Ordination. As such, we are persons living within a vibrant Christian community inspired by the love of Christ.

The minister as shepherd, rather than relying on his own power, must "labor, striving according to His power, which mightily works within me."[33] In this regard, the shepherd as doctor heals and brings people closer to God through the process of deification.[34] To do this effectively, healing must occur in the heart of both the minister and the people he is called to serve. Similarly, the shepherd as teacher must be trained properly and continue to grow towards deification throughout his entire ministry. Faced with Christ's unparalleled humility, the minister

---

[29] 1 Timothy 4:12 NKJV.

[30] Allen, *Ministry of the Church*, 42.

[31] Matthew 5:13-14 NKJV.

[32] John 8:12 KJV.

[33] Colossians 1:29 NASB.

[34] Allen, *Ministry of the Church*, 74.

must place humility first in his heart whether he serves in a local church or monastery. Regardless of the venue, the minister as shepherd cares for both the spiritual and bodily needs of his flock by loving God with his whole heart, mind, soul, and strength and loving his neighbor as himself.

What keeps us from embracing this labor of love? Why do we stubbornly cling to our sinful selfishness? "The essence of the fall of man is pride."[35] Our sin is a form of idolatry by which "man refuses to refer created being to communion with God."[36] A rupture between being and communion ensues,[37] and we live as individuals centered on self and divorced from God and others. True humility opens our hearts to perfect love. It is both spiritually and scripturally sound that when Jesus was asked about the greatest commandment, He did not hesitate in challenging us to both love God and love our neighbor.[38] "Every therapeutic issue in spiritual direction comes down in some way or another to *love*."[39] Because "God is love,"[40] the priest offers God's love.

---

[35] Clark Carlton, *The Life: The Orthodox Doctrine of Salvation* (Salisbury, MA: Regina Orthodox Press, 2000), 164.

[36] John D. Zizioulas, *Being as Communion* (Crestwood, NY: St. Vladimir's Seminary Press, 1985), 102.

[37] Ibid.

[38] Matthew 22:37-40.

[39] Joseph J. Allen, *Inner Way* (Brookline, MA: Holy Cross Orthodox Press, 2000), 90 (emphasis in original).

[40] 1 John 4:8 NKJV.

The Kingdom of God is more real, more present, and more powerful than what we see with our eyes and touch with our physical hands. We find God is the deepest part of ourselves. "One's inner person – his or her depths – serves as a conduit for the flow of God's grace."[41] Several decades ago, I attended a workshop where the distinction between our Christ-self and our false-self was made. Our false-self is who we are on the surface, with us in charge of our lives, revealing our most selfish selves. Our Christ-self, on the other hand, is who we are deep down inside. Our Christ-self is who God calls us to be, our deified self where we begin to become "partakers of the divine nature."[42] God's grace touches us in this deepest part of ourselves. It is in "the place of the heart" that "God and human beings meet in the experiences of the covenantal life."[43]

The very name of Emmanuel loudly proclaims that God is indeed with us. By being present in our everyday lives, God immerses Himself in our suffering. God fully understands our pain and works "with us to bring forth all possible good from the evil we are suffering."[44] In the Old Testament, Joseph told his brothers that what they meant for evil, God turned into "good, to save many people alive."[45] In the New Testament, Paul reminds us that the Lord works for the good of those both loving Him and

---

[41] Allen, *Inner Way*, 4.
[42] 2 Peter 1:4, NASB.
[43] Allen, *Inner Way*, 96.
[44] Ibid., 88.
[45] Genesis 50:20 NKJV.

"called according to His purpose."[46] The Cross of Christ reveals God's infinite immersion into our pain and suffering. Because God meets us in our suffering, He offers us hope. Whenever the priest helps people cope with their pain and face their suffering, he points them towards God.

We are reminded to live the Virtue of Humility every Monday. Whether at home or at work, to the extent we imitate our Saviour and let His presence permeate our lives, we strive to serve rather than being served and in so doing put the needs of others before our own. This is a great way to begin a busy and challenging workweek whatever our calling.

....

[46] Romans 8:28 NASB.

CHAPTER TWO

TUESDAY

THE VIRTUE OF PURITY

"Blessed are the pure in heart, for they shall see God" (Matthew 5:8 NASB).

Our workweek continues with the most precious desire in our hearts, the eternal quest to see and experience our Triune God. The Virtue of Purity seeks its earliest expression in our childhood faith. I remember being about seven years old and visiting the Cathedral of the Immaculate Conception in downtown Fort Wayne for the Benediction of the Blessed Sacrament with Mom and Dad. It was nighttime, and the magnificent church was nearly empty, but the Blessed Sacrament stood boldly in its gold, shiny monstrance on the huge altar deep in the sanctuary. The great cathedral, only partially lit and nearly empty, displayed a quiet magnificence, the perfect resting place for our humble adoration of the Corpus Christi.

Linking my Roman Catholic childhood to my current Orthodox faith, I remain struck by the stark contrast between the magnificent cathedral and the humble

Host. Back in the old days, we entered a church with deep reverence, and the cathedral was, like the Jewish temple in Jesus' day, the home of the Living God. "And he said, Draw not nigh hither: put off thy shoes from off thy feet, for the place whereon thou standest is holy ground."[47] But that night, though Mom, Dad, and I were among the few there present, the hearts of the faithful though comfortable in the quiet cathedral were focused on the humble Host housed in the golden monstrance. We willingly bent our knees before the most ultimate mystery of our Roman Catholic faith. "Adoration is perhaps the Western devotion that most perfectly embodies and expresses the essence of our Orthodox Life."[48] The church was boldly magnificent, but at the heart of our faith stood the Body of Christ in silent simplicity. Indeed, "the Sacred Mysteries truly are the Body and Blood of our Lord."[49]

I was blessed with sixteen wonder-filled years of Catholic education, spanning eight years at Saint Charles Borromeo Church and School, four years at Bishop Dwenger High School, and four years at the University of Notre Dame. My educational journey began at Saint Charles, and our nuns were both kind and generous in their love for the Lord and their young charges. Our week began each Sunday with morning Mass. One of my earliest childhood memories was being allowed to stand on the

---

[47] Exodus 3:5 KJV.

[48] Patrick Cardine, "Benediction-Adoration: A Beautiful Vision," in The Orthodox West, https://www.orthodoxwest.com/beautiful-vision (accessed May 2, 2018).

[49] Ibid.

back of the pew in front of us, held in place by Mom, so I could see the action around the altar better. The Mass was still in Latin, as the changes of Vatican II were soon to be implemented. The priest faced away from us by facing the altar, towards God, in essence leading the congregation to God in our worship. The whole Mass experience, from the foreign language to the magnificent statues to the giant crucifix above the Holy Altar, was shrouded in a most magnificent mystery. Heaven was unimaginable, hell was real, and both purgatory and limbo made sense. We were a people of the Cross, reminded of our penitential position during Lent and Good Friday, experiencing the joyful Resurrection on the first day of the week.

While immersed in our faith, we experienced a deep and abiding peace arising from the apparent certainty of our beliefs. We ate fish on Friday and did not wonder why. We marveled at the Baby Jesus with Mary and Joseph in the Grotto at church and loved the colorful lights of the Christmas tree and the bountiful presents under this tree at home. We willingly surrendered something fun during Lent. We laid low all day on Good Friday while visiting church sometime between noon and 3:00 p.m. to remember and reverence Christ's suffering on the Cross. Yet as children we knew deep down inside the Resurrection of Jesus and some chocolate Easter bunnies were just around the corner.

Our life was sacramental and filled with mystery: Confession in second grade, Communion in third grade, and Confirmation in fourth grade. I was baptized at Saint Patrick Catholic Church in Chesterton, Indiana, very soon after birth. Little did I know I would receive the Holy Chrism as an Orthodox convert fifty-six years later at Saint Patrick Orthodox Church in Bealeton, Virginia. I went to Confession in second grade and received my first Holy Communion in third. Our sins were little but seemed big to us. One day I raised my eyebrows to say hi to Patricia, a girl I had a crush on, and I felt guilty for the committing the "sin" of making "goo-goo" eyes at a girl. I remember one Confession, being so relieved to be forgiven for a sin I don't even recall, but walking up the church aisle back to my pew so filled with joy because my feeling bad at the burden of this particular sin was lifted away forever. The black spots dotting our white souls were cleansed and removed through the Sacrament of Confession. "As far as the east is from the west, so far hath he removed our transgressions from us."[50] Just as Confession was held in the cramped darkness and anonymity of the confessional, Holy Communion was bold and bright, the sacrament of light. We knelt at the communion rail in joyful anticipation of receiving the actual Body of Christ.

As a child I loved my black Saint Joseph's Missal. One Sunday an African priest from overseas visited our church, and I asked him for his autograph, and he signed my missal in the church parking lot after Mass. Sitting in the classroom at Saint Charles School one sunny day, as we struggled through our daily lessons, I recall looking out the window and seeing Father Edward Hessian, our senior parish priest, dressed in comfortable outdoors

---

[50] Psalm 103:12 KVJ.

clothes and loading the trunk of his car. It looked like he was going fishing! As a young child, I could not imagine a better life than being a priest.

The holiness and joy of church life touched the deepest part of our hearts. With Jesus and Mary as our best friends, we instinctively and easily experienced an ongoing union and communion with God.

Immersed in our neighborhood church and school, our lives seemed inseparable from God. "For I am convinced that neither death, nor life, nor angels, nor rulers, nor things present, nor things to come, nor powers, nor height, nor depth, nor anything else in all creation, will be able to separate us from the love of God in Christ Jesus our Lord."[51] Through this childlike communion with Christ, with nothing to separate us from His infinite love, we instinctively sought God's will for our lives.

Our devout priests at Saint Charles Catholic Church were our heroes. Saint John Chrysostom declares the priest "must be as pure as if he were standing in heaven itself" because his ministry though "done on earth… is ranked among heavenly ordinances."[52] Pastoral care requires both the complete commitment of the shepherd and the love and respect of the flock.[53] Saint Ambrose calls upon the priest to help others without harming them.[54] Saint Gregory the Great reminds the priest to be "pure in thought" as he accepts the challenge "of wiping away

---

[51] Romans 8:38-39 NRSV.
[52] Allen, *The Ministry of the Church: The Image of Pastoral Care*, 99.
[53] Ibid., 118.
[54] Ibid., 120.

the stains of pollution in the hearts of others."⁵⁵ Saint Ephraim the Syrian directs the shepherd to the example of Jesus Christ who "gave himself up for the sake of the sheep."⁵⁶ Saint Gregory of Nyssa explains how "a priest of hidden mysteries" is changed deep down inside by the Holy Spirit as "his invisible soul is changed for the better by a certain invisible power and grace."⁵⁷ Finally, Saint Cyril of Alexandria teaches that Jesus the "Great Shepherd" ordains the priest through the Holy Spirit and as a result "the shepherd serves in the ministry of the Lord Jesus himself."⁵⁸ Truly the priest as shepherd serves his flock not in and of himself, "but I labored even more than all of them, yet not I, but the grace of God with me."⁵⁹

Saint Antony the Great of Egypt, the father of hermits, lived in the second and third centuries. Saint Athanasius wrote his famous *Life of Antony* in 360 and said this of the great ascetic: "It was not his physical dimensions that distinguished him from the rest, but the stability of character and the purity of the soul."⁶⁰ As a young man, Saint Antony heard the Gospel account of the rich young

---

[55] Ibid., 121.
[56] Ibid., 122.
[57] Ibid., 123.
[58] Ibid.
[59] 1 Corinthians 15:10b (NASB).
[60] Saint Athanasius, *The Life of Antony and the Letter to Marcellinus*, translated by Robert Gregg (Mahwah, NJ: Paulist Press, 1980), 81.

man.[61] He took these words to heart and immediately began selling his possessions.[62] "The state of his soul was one of purity."[63]

The sacramental life of the Church immerses us in this purity. Our embrace of purity begins at the moment Christ embraces us in the Sacrament of Baptism. "Go therefore and make disciples of all the nations, baptizing them in the name of the Father and of the Son and of the Holy Spirit."[64] With this command, the Risen Christ proclaims the baptismal blessing in its Trinitarian formulation, with the three persons of the Holy Trinity professed. Saint Basil the Great describes faith and baptism as two means of salvation and declares: "For as we believe in the Father, Son, and Holy Spirit, so also are we baptized in the name of the Father, Son, and Holy Spirit."[65]

The Holy Spirit cleaves to a person at the moment of Baptism.[66] Baptism confers being and initiates our existence in Christ.[67] The newly-baptized believer in Christ is "buried with Him in baptism, in which you also were

---

[61] Matthew 19:21.

[62] Saint Athanasius, *The Life of Antony and the Letter to Marcellinus*, 31.

[63] Ibid., 42.

[64] Matthew 28:19 NKJV.

[65] Saint Basil, *On the Holy Spirit*, translated by Stephen Hildebrand (Yonkers, NY: St. Vladimir's Seminary Press, 2011), 59.

[66] Georgios Mantzaridis, *The Deification of Man* (Crestwood, NY: St. Vladimir's Seminary Press, 1984), 31.

[67] Nicholas Cabasilas, *The Life in Christ*, translated by Carmino J. deCatanzaro (Crestwood, NY: St. Vladimir's Seminary Press, 1974), 49.

raised with Him through faith in the working of God, who raised Him from the dead."[68] The anointing with Holy Chrism "perfects (the new believer) who has received [new] birth by infusing into him the energy that befits such a life."[69] Filled with the Holy Spirit, the newly-anointed Orthodox Christian believer encounters life in a strikingly different way. "Therefore we have been buried with Him through baptism into death, so that as Christ was raised from the dead through the glory of the Father, so we too might walk in newness of life."[70] With these words, Saint Paul describes the heart of Baptism, our dying with Christ, our death to sin, and our resurrection with Christ into new life, "dead indeed to sin, but alive to God in Christ Jesus our Lord."[71]

Baptisms abound during the feast of Pascha, the feast of feasts. "The center of the church year is the triumphant celebration of Pascha, which marks the victory of Christ over death, and therefore our own release from slavery to sin, sickness, and death."[72] Just as Baptism transforms us from death to life, Pascha or passage from death to new life into the Kingdom of God allows us to participate in the life, death, and resurrection of Jesus Christ in a way transforming our hearts and our world.[73]

---

[68] Colossians 2:12 NKJV.
[69] Cabasilas, *The Life in Christ*, 50.
[70] Romans 6:4 NASB.
[71] Romans 6:11 NKJV.
[72] Paul Meyendorff, *The Anointing of the Sick* (Crestwood, NY: St. Vladimir's Seminary Press, 2009), 28.
[73] Alexander Schmemann, *Of Water & the Spirit* (Crestwood, New

The Holy Spirit lies at the very heart of the divine revelation and the Christian life and dwells inside each believer. To know, to receive, and to be in communion with the Holy Spirit is the Church's ultimate mystery. The fulfillment of Baptism in the holy anointing is the personal coming of the Holy Spirit as the Holy Spirit Himself abides in the believer.[74] We know the Holy Spirit not from books but by His presence within us,[75] leading to the fruit of the Holy Spirit, including love, joy, and peace.[76] Our new life in Christ is not another life, or a different life, but the same life renewed, transformed, and transfigured by the Holy Spirit.[77]

Saint Basil in his classic work *On the Holy Spirit* emphasizes "how in everything the Holy Spirit is indivisible and inseparable from the Father and the Son."[78] "The key term of *On the Holy Spirit* is *koinonia* (communion): the Holy Spirit participates in the life of the Father and the Son."[79] There is an indescribable communion between the three persons of the Trinity. The Holy Spirit "is joined through the one Son to the one Father, and through himself, he completes the famed and blessed Trinity."[80]

York: St. Vladimir's Seminary Press, 1974), 38.

[74] Ibid., 104.

[75] Ibid., 105.

[76] Galatians 5:22.

[77] Schmemann, *Of Water & the Spirit*, 107.

[78] Saint Basil, *On the Holy Spirit*, 69.

[79] Boris Bobrinskoy, *The Mystery of the Trinity* (Crestwood, New York: St. Vladimir's Seminary Press, 1999), 244.

[80] Saint Basil, *On the Holy Spirit*, 81.

The Holy Spirit "existed, and pre-existed, and co-existed with the Father and the Son before the ages."[81] As such, all three persons in the Holy Trinity participated in creation. The Father and the Holy Spirit are mentioned in the beginning of Genesis: "In the beginning God created the heaven and the earth. … And the Spirit of God moved upon the face of the waters."[82] In a similar way, the beginning of John's Gospel brings the Son into the act of creation: "In the beginning was the Word, and the Word was with God, and the Word was God. He was in the beginning with God. All things were made through Him, and without Him nothing was made that was made."[83] The creative action of the Trinity is especially pronounced in the creation of the heavenly angels. "You would learn the communion of the Spirit with the Father and the Son also from what was created in the beginning, for the pure, intelligent, and other-worldly powers both are and are called holy because they have acquired holiness as a gift given to them by the Holy Spirit."[84] Reflecting upon creation, one perceives the interaction of the Holy Trinity: "the initial cause of their existence (the Father), the Maker (the Son), the Perfecter (the Spirit)."[85] Within creation "the source of being is one, which makes through the Son, and which perfects in the Spirit."[86]

---

[81] Ibid., 85.
[82] Genesis 1:1,2b KJV.
[83] John 1:1-3 NKJV.
[84] Saint Basil, *On the Holy Spirit*, 70.
[85] Ibid., 70-71.
[86] Ibid., 71.

The divine nature of the Holy Spirit cannot be comprehended by our finite minds. "The excellence of his nature is known not only from the fact that he has the same titles as the Father and the Son and that he shares in their work but also from the fact that like them he is beyond comprehension."[87] Just as words cannot adequately describe God the Father in His essence, so too is the divinity of God the Son and God the Holy Spirit both indescribable and incomprehensible. "For what the Lord says about the Father, that he is beyond human thought, and what he says about the Son, these very things he says also about the Holy Spirit."[88]

According to Professor Stephen Hildebrand of Franciscan University of Steubenville, "To explain how the Father and the Son, as unique *hypostaseis*, are not two Gods, Basil invokes the archetype-image metaphor."[89] In this regard, if God the Father is the archetype, God the Son "is the image of the invisible God, the firstborn over all creation."[90] The Holy Spirit is present whenever we fix our gaze on the Son, the image of the invisible and unseen Father: "When through his illuminating power we fix our eyes on the beauty of the image of the unseen God, and through the image are led up to the more than beautiful vision of the archetype, his Spirit of knowledge is somehow inseparably present."[91] In this regard, Jesus

---

[87] Ibid., 91.

[88] Ibid.

[89] Stephen Hildebrand, "Introduction," in Ibid., 24.

[90] Colossians 1:15 NKJV.

[91] Saint Basil, *On the Holy Spirit*, 82.

tells the Samaritan woman at the well, "God *is* a spirit: and they that worship him must worship *him* in spirit and in truth."[92] In other words, "just as we speak of worship in the Son as worship in the Image of God the Father, so also we speak of worship in the Spirit as worship in him who manifests the divinity of the Lord. Therefore, in worship the Holy Spirit is inseparable from the Father and the Son."[93]

"Now the greatest sign of the Spirit's union with the Father and the Son is that he is said to be related to God as our spirit is to each of us."[94] Each person of the Trinity is unique. "The way, then, to knowledge of God is from the one Spirit, through the one Son, to the one Father. And conversely the goodness and holiness by nature and the royal dignity reach from the Father, through the Only-begotten, to the Spirit. In this way the persons are confessed and the pious dogma of the monarchy does not fall away."[95]

"There are, therefore, two movements of the Trinitarian grace, descending and ascending. The two movements – the ascending one, that is, knowledge and adoration, on the one hand, and furthermore, the descending one, the sanctification of man by Trinitarian grace – always occurs *through* the Spirit and *in* the Spirit."[96] We ascend towards God with knowledge and adoration, and the grace of God

---

[92] John 4:24 KJV.

[93] Saint Basil, *On the Holy Spirit*, 103.

[94] Ibid., 75.

[95] Ibid., 83.

[96] Bobrinskoy, *The Mystery of the Trinity*, 238 (emphasis in original).

descends to us as we strive to live pure and holy lives. This mutual love is accomplished through and in the Holy Spirit.

"Basil associates the Spirit chiefly with the work of sanctification and the inculcation of Christian virtue."[97] The word "Holy" applies in a special way to each Person of the Holy Trinity. Just "as the Father is holy and as the Son is holy," so too "for the Spirit, holiness is an essential part of his nature, so that he is not made holy but makes holy."[98] In a similar way, Saint Basil cites Sacred Scripture in considering two names of the Holy Spirit and how these names relate to the Father and the Son. " 'God is Spirit' (Jn 4.24). 'The Spirit of our face, Christ the Lord' (Lam 4.20)."[99] Throughout Sacred Scripture, the names of God the Father and His Only-begotten Son apply similarly to the third person within the Holy Trinity. "Thus the names of the Father and the Son are common to the Spirit who has these names because of his kinship in nature."[100] We live pure lives to the extent we allow the Holy Spirit to direct our actions and the Holy Trinity to reign in our hearts.

As we focus all day Tuesday on the Virtue of Purity, we imagine the power and presence of the Most Holy Trinity in our hearts and lives as He has worked in the lives of the

---

[97] Christopher A. Beeley, *Gregory of Nazianzus on the Trinity and the Knowledge of God* (New York: Oxford University Press, 2008), 298.

[98] Saint Basil, *On the Holy Spirit*, 84.

[99] Ibid.

[100] Ibid.

saints and continues to work in the hearts of our priests, deacons, subdeacons, monks and nuns, and all the people of God. God our loving Father, Jesus our Lord and Savior, and the indwelling Holy Spirit inspire us to embrace the Virtue of Purity every minute during this second day of our workweek.

CHAPTER THREE

WEDNESDAY

THE VIRTUE OF HOLINESS

Finally, brethren, whatever is true, whatever is honorable,
whatever is right, whatever is pure, whatever is lovely,
whatever is of good repute, if there is
any excellence and if anything worthy
of praise, dwell on these things
(Philippians 4:8 NASB).

Wednesday is referred to affectionately across America as "hump day" by many workers. In the middle of a grueling workweek, by day's end we will have passed the halfway point towards a relaxing weekend with family and friends. Midweek seems like an opportune time to embrace the Virtue of Holiness. Holiness begins with a heart committed to compassionate service.

During my memorable junior year at the University of Notre Dame, besides watching quarterback Joe Montana lead the Fighting Irish to a national championship at the Cotton Bowl, I enrolled in the best course of my college career. The class entitled Theology and Community Service brought us to a local nursing home to minister to the elderly. Though published in book form later, one of the few college textbooks I still possess is *Compassion* written by Roman Catholic priests Father Henri Nouwen and Father Don McNeill, the latter my professor for the course, and Doug Morrison. What was especially memorable about this course was how we as a class read the book *Compassion* in manuscript form. I took the class about four years before the book was published. It was great as undergrads to serve as guinea pigs for the authors as they put the finishing touches on their draft work in progress. The main theme of this college course is summarized best by this short passage from the book: "Compassion asks us to go where it hurts, to enter into places of pain, to share in brokenness, fear, confusion, and anguish. Compassion challenges us to cry out with those in misery, to mourn with those who are lonely, to weep with those in tears. Compassion requires us to be weak with the weak, vulnerable with the vulnerable, and powerless with the powerless. Compassion means full immersion in the condition of being human."[101]

I visited Iris (real name) and Joe (pseudonym), two elderly residents at a South Bend, Indiana, nursing home, as part of this college course. I still recall vividly the strong smell of decay as I walked through the front door for my initial visit. I walked into Joe's room first. He sat on the edge of his bed in a gloomy room and let stream a veritable litany of complaints against the nursing home. He

---

[101] Henri J. M. Nouwen, Donald P. McNeill, and Douglas A. Morrison, *Compassion* (New York: Doubleday, 1982), 4.

hated living there, the staff treated them all "like dirt," and their food was like garbage, he wouldn't feed it "to the pigs." After this depressing visit, I walked down the hall and entered Iris' bright room. A cheerful woman with a memorable porcelain dog, Iris loved the Lord and enjoyed talking about Jesus. I asked her about her nursing home experiences. She loved it there. The nurses and orderlies treated the residents "like kings and queens." Every meal was like "a feast." When hit with hard times as a young woman, at a point of near despair, doing dishes at the kitchen sink, Iris received an insight from deep down inside, "There's always darkness before the dawn." She laughed at the time and felt an immediate, intense, and immense joy; her life was never the same.

I went to the nursing home to serve but learned a very valuable secret that day. Iris taught me by her example the inherent joy of being a Christian. Joe taught me by this pessimistic approach to life the pertinent power of a positive attitude. At the crossroads of suffering and pain, a person can choose to get better or bitter. Iris heeded Saint Paul's advice and "learned to be content whatever the circumstances."[102] Poor Joe's discontent unnecessarily added to his suffering.

As a career educator, each year I share the story of Iris and Joe with my grade school children. I ask them to consider when precisely in the lives of these two elderly people their respective attitudes of either joy or despair began. Students eagerly raise their hands and guess dif-

---

[102] Philippians 4:11 NLT.

ferent ages. Although the answers vary widely, with some students believing these attitudes took root in Iris and Joe during middle or old age, others think this may have happened when they were much younger, perhaps as early as grade school. Granted we cannot know for sure, yet it seems possible if not likely Joe in his childhood hated his school, disliked his teachers, and complained about the cafeteria food. Iris may have expressed the very opposite attitude at the exact same age: loving her school, liking her teachers, and enjoying school lunches. As elderly residents at a nursing home during their challenging golden years, Iris may have recalled her optimistic life experiences and decided to make things better. Joe, on the other hand, may have fallen back into a lifetime pattern of pessimism and chose to be bitter. These two roads, to become better or bitter, remain open to each of us while facing an array of challenging circumstances.

"In theology, *compassion* means that the sufferer is 'grasped' by one who 'co-passionates.'"[103] To be compassionate towards others, we must be in touch with our own mutual suffering. By "remaining in touch with his own experiences of suffering, sinfulness, and limitations,"[104] an elder could share these attributes with the person being ministered to, walking with him or her into the places of pain together. The one wounded no longer faces suffering alone.

---

[103] Allen, *Inner Way*, 83 (emphasis in original).
[104] Ibid.

One of my college roommates at Notre Dame suddenly lost his father during the Christmas break of our freshman year. I felt sad at his loss and expressed my condolences. Yet it was only several years later as I held the hand of my own beloved father as he breathed his last in his valiant battle against cancer that I knew what it truly meant to lose one's dad. My ability to share the pain of a friend losing a parent became exponentially greater after my own dad died.

To enter the places of pain and truly listen to and experience the suffering shared by others, we need to be in touch with our own pain and suffering. Within a therapeutic context, "*empathy* helps healing to occur because the patient feels that his or her counselor is truly capable of entering his frame and perspective."[105] Although we can never fully understand another person's unique experience of pain and suffering, our ability to empathize with others is enhanced to the degree we have faced and accepted our own pain and suffering. By becoming one of us and dying on the Cross, Jesus offered humanity the ability to once again be reborn in the image and likeness of God through the power of love.

Whatever our vocation, we move closer to the holiness of our Triune God to the extent we love God and love our neighbor in everything we do. "To care for people is to share their joy and sorrow, their hope and despair, their triumph and defeat."[106] I feel a deep and abiding call to

---

[105] Ibid., (emphasis in original).
[106] Joseph J. Allen, ed., *And He Leads Them* (Ben Lomond, CA: Conciliar Press, 2001), 244.

the priesthood. As I reflect on my past pastoral ministry experiences and discern God's call in my life, these words of His Eminence Metropolitan Philip of thrice-blessed memory are most inspiring. "Priesthood is not a job; it is a *vocation*. Priesthood is not a profession; it is a covenant between the priest and his parish."[107]

Just as the incarnate Christ was fully God and fully man, both God and bondservant, so too are we called to bring the light of Jesus our God into the hearts of hurting people, uniting the divine with the human. The priest's mission is to lead His people to Jesus. As Metropolitan Philip told his priests, "You were ordained in order to bring Christ to people and people to Christ."[108] This mission begun by the priest is passed to each of his people. Our young people at Saint Patrick Orthodox Church fulfill this mission regularly by enthusiastically engaging in ministry ventures to benefit our local community. Rather than performing ministry from a sense of duty, our youth engage in a variety of communal outreaches with an enthusiasm grounded in their love of Christ and friendship with Mary. With this emphasis, our young people see their very joyful "love of God" and "love of neighbor" intertwining and permeating their pastoral ministry experiences. Whether scrubbing and painting the new home for a destitute family or talking with the poor children from these residences while bringing boxes of gifts just before Christmas, our youth in giving

---

[107] Ibid., (emphasis in original).
[108] Joseph J. Allen, ed., *Orthodox Synthesis: The Unity of Theological Thought* (Crestwood, NY: St. Vladimir's Seminary Press, 1981), 95.

of themselves experience the joy of Jesus. They take to their community what they learn at St. Patrick Orthodox Church as acolytes and choir members, attending our Divine Liturgies and living in sound Orthodox homes, and their rich Orthodox experiences become a part of who they are deep down inside. Truly "it is only with the heart that one can see rightly; what is essential is invisible to the eye."[109] Imitating Jesus, our young people become joyful bondservants of Christ. Truly "one cannot speak of theology and praxis as if they were different, but rather of *theological praxis*."[110] For these Orthodox youth, theory and praxis, theology and practice, merge into one. From this seed of compassion springs the bud of holiness.

Both for our youth and for every Orthodox believer, "divine grace and human act are *both* required."[111] "And for this purpose also I labor, striving according to His power, which mightily works within me."[112] This interaction between the divine and human inside every Orthodox Christian believer defines true beauty. "The awful thing is that beauty is mysterious as well as terrible. God and the devil are fighting there and the battlefield is the heart of man."[113] With these words, Russian author Fyo-

---

[109] Saint-Exupéry, *The Little Prince*, 73.

[110] Allen, *Orthodox Synthesis*, 99 (emphasis in original).

[111] Ibid., 102 (emphasis in original).

[112] Colossians 1:29 NASB.

[113] Fyodor Dostoevsky, *The Brothers Karamazov*, translated by Constance Garnett, in *Great Books of the Western World*, vol. 52 (Chicago: Encyclopaedia Britannica, 1952), 54.

dor Dostoevsky aptly describes the incessant obstacles involved in man's quest for holiness.

Angels and demons accompany us along this journey. "There are all sorts of monsters to be met with on the way, and the monsters are not devils, they are not our neighbour, they are just ourselves."[114] The inward life is where we find God as much as humanly possible, but we must first face and walk past our own monsters. The monsters deep down inside are not to be destroyed or vanquished but only can be overcome by being understood and embraced. The monsters call us to become our better selves and in so doing both reveal our inner strength and teach us humility. This humility clears a narrow path into the lifelong pursuit of holiness. The inward life cannot begin until we face and embrace the monsters within.

We face these inner monsters and begin the trek towards holiness within the friendly confines of the Orthodox Church. "For by these He has granted to us His precious and magnificent promises, in order that by them you might become partakers of *the* divine nature, having escaped the corruption that is in the world by lust."[115] We partake of the divine nature through the Holy Orthodox Church, specifically through our participation in the Divine Liturgy.

The Divine Liturgy provides the best example of how we live our rich Orthodox theology experientially. For example, we come into direct contact with God by receiving

---

[114] Bloom, *Beginning to Pray*, 67.
[115] 2 Peter 1:4 NASB.

the Holy Eucharist each Sunday and Feast Day. "Through the Holy Eucharist, we are transformed into that which we receive."[116] The baptized, though many in number, are united as one body in the Eucharistic celebration.[117] "Because there is one bread, we who are many are one body, for we all partake of the one bread."[118] The Eucharist involves a sacrificial offering.[119] Saint Cyprian describes the Eucharist as the offering of a sacrifice by Christ our high priest.[120] Yet "if we sin willfully after we have received the knowledge of the truth, there no longer remains a sacrifice for sins."[121] Whereas Baptism and Confession involve our conversion and *metanoia* through repentance and a change of heart, the Eucharist commemorates Christ's work of salvation.[122]

Through our union and communion with Christ, with nothing to separate us from His infinite love, we seek His will for our lives. The priest, in imitation of Christ, proclaims the words of institution during the Canon of the Mass, and the bread and wine become the

---

[116] Christoforos Stavropouplos, *Partakers of Divine Nature* (Minneapolis, MN: Light and Life Publishing, 1976), 59.

[117] Veselin Kesich, *The Birth of the Church: AD 33-200*, in The Church in History, vol.1, part 1, *Formation and Struggles* (Crestwood, NY: St. Vladimir's Seminary Press, 2007), 93.

[118] 1 Corinthians 10:17 NRSV.

[119] Williston Walker, Richard Norris, David Lotz, and Robert Handy, *A History of the Christian Church*, 4th ed. (New York: Scribner, 1985), 109.

[120] Ibid., 110.

[121] Hebrews 10:26 NKJV.

[122] Walker *et al*, *A History of the Christian Church*, 109-110.

Body and Blood of Christ through the power of the Holy Spirit.

Just as the Orthodox Church is the Body of Christ, "Orthodox spirituality is also Christ-centred, since only within the Church can we come into communion with Christ."[123] Besides our most wonder-filled Divine Liturgy, our union and communion with God grows to the extent we immerse ourselves in Sacred Scripture, the Sacraments, and the lives of the saints.

According to Metropolitan Athanasios of Limassol, "The Holy Bible is purely a spiritual text that speaks about God's energy in the world."[124] In other words, "Holy Scripture is not the revelation, but the word about the revelation, which helps Christians to progress towards deification and sanctification."[125] This revelation is Jesus Christ, the Incarnate God-man conquering sin and death through His life-giving Cross and Resurrection. The entire Bible, both Old and New Testaments, points to Jesus Christ and His offer of salvation. In the Old Testament, God created us in His image and likeness. "Humanity was created in the image of God, and each

---

[123] Metropolitan Hierotheos of Nafpaktos, *Orthodox Spirituality*, 5th ed., translated by Effie Mavromichali (Levadia, Greece: Birth of the Theotokos Monastery, 2008), 21.

[124] Kyriacos Markides, *Gifts of the Desert* (New York: Doubleday, 2005), 92.

[125] Metropolitan Hierotheos of Nafpaktos, *Hesychia and Theology: The Context for Man's Healing in the Orthodox Church*, translated by Sister Pelagia Selfe (Levadia, Greece: Birth of the Theotokos Monastery, 2007), 203.

and every human being is called to become like God."[126] In the New Testament, after "the Word became flesh and dwelt among us,"[127] our new life in Christ could begin because after the Cross and Resurrection, Jesus returned to the Father as God and man. For this reason, "The divine Incarnation brings us again to the Father and presents us with the potential of realizing 'the likeness' of God in our lives."[128]

Besides sharing the truth of Sacred Scripture, the Orthodox Church as the Body of Christ offers us the Sacraments as the means to guide us to the *telos* of union and communion with God. "Through the Sacraments, the uncreated grace and energy of God enters our heart."[129] Our journey begins with Baptism and Chrismation, reborn in water and sealed with the Holy Chrism. "Our spirit wears the Saviour Christ as a garment, an incorruptible uniform worthy of the Holy Spirit which has granted us rebirth and sealed us in a new style of living."[130] Despite this rebirth, we still fall short and sin, missing the mark often as the world vies for our attention and devotion. After sin happens, the Orthodox Church offers repentance and forgiveness through the Sacrament of Confession. Father Maximos describes Confession as "nothing but a method to help us take a good look at our real self."[131] Faced with

---

[126] Stavropouplos, *Partakers of Divine Nature*, 23.

[127] John 1:14 NASB.

[128] Stavropouplos, *Partakers of Divine Nature*, 29.

[129] Hierotheos, *Orthodox Spirituality*, 66.

[130] Stavropouplos, *Partakers of Divine Nature*, 47.

[131] Markides, *Gifts of the Desert*, 335.

the self-love of our false self, we can repent and discover our Christ-self, the very self God calls us to become deep down inside. "Repentance causes tears to bubble up from the depths of the soul. These tears cleanse the heart and wipe away great sins."[132] Freed from the despair of sin and the fear of death, we can fill ourselves more with God.

Perhaps the very best way to receive God is through the Holy Eucharist. "When a person receives the holy Sacrament, he receives concurrently the promise of an indescribable communion with Christ in the age to come."[133] Metropolitan Athanasios' magnificent retelling of the life of Saint Paisios the Great, not eating for seventy-two years yet still keeping "himself alive only with Holy Communion,"[134] aptly describes the present and eschatological power of the Holy Eucharist in our lives.

From Baptism and Chrismation to Confession and Communion, we continually learn how to partake of the divine nature. Saint Paisios is but one of a great cloud of witnesses.

The lives of the saints offer us a final path towards holiness. "The saints are holy because they are united with God Who is holy, and because they share in His uncreated grace."[135] This holiness is not seen in one or two aspects within the lives of the saints but permeates their entire existence, both body and soul. "A person is made up of

---

[132] Stavropouplos, *Partakers of Divine Nature*, 53.

[133] Ibid., 66.

[134] Markides, *Gifts of the Desert*, 236.

[135] Hierotheos, *Hesychia and Theology: The Context for Man's Healing in the Orthodox Church*, 38

body and soul, which co-exist without any confusion."[136] When both body and soul live fully for God, participation in His divine nature becomes possible. In other words, "a Saint is someone who partakes, in varying degrees, in the uncreated grace of God, and especially in the deifying grace and energy of God."[137] Simply stated, the holy saints within the Orthodox Church live now with God in heaven because they learned how to pray and to love here on earth.

We like the saints strive to partake of the divine nature within the Orthodox Church by celebrating the Divine Liturgy, immersing ourselves in God's Word and participating in the Holy Sacraments. Our journey of love begins with a humble prayer focused on God: "The God who is totally unknowable in the sphere of human knowledge, He who is unapproachable in His essence, is revealed to the heart which loves Him. The revelation takes place in mystical silence."[138] We experience the energy of God and partake in His divine nature in this mystical silence discovered deep within the recesses of our hearts.

This ongoing quest to become "partakers of the divine nature"[139] touches every aspect of our lives. As creatures, we never can attain full union and communion with the divine essence. Whereas we are creatures, God is, has been, and always will be uncreated. Yet we still may partake in the divine nature through our union with the

---

[136] Hierotheos, *Orthodox Spirituality*, 33.

[137] Ibid., 20.

[138] Stavropouplos, *Partakers of Divine Nature*, 83.

[139] 2 Peter 1:4 NASB.

divine energies. Within Orthodox theology, the uncreated Christ possesses both a hypostatic union with His divine nature and a substantial union within the Trinity.[140] As created beings, we obtain neither hypostatic nor substantial union with God: our union occurs within the realm of the divine energies. This union by grace makes us participants in the divine nature, through the divine energies, without losing our essence in the divine essence of God.[141] Just as Christ remained God while becoming man through the mystery of the Incarnation, we "remain creatures while becoming God by grace."[142] Through the process of deification, we are not god by nature, but merely a created god, a god by grace or by status.[143]

"The Word of God came in His own Person, because it was He alone, the Image of the Father, Who could recreate man made after the image."[144] Mired in sin, sickness, and death, humanity longs for forgiveness, wholeness, and life. "For we know that the whole creation groans and suffers the pains of childbirth together until now."[145] The Incarnation, "the Word became flesh,"[146] changes everything.

---

[140] Vladimir Lossky, *The Mystical Theology of the Eastern Church* (Crestwood, NY: St. Vladimir's Seminary Press, 1976), 87.

[141] Ibid.

[142] Ibid.

[143] Timothy Ware, *The Orthodox Church* (London: Penguin Books, 1997), 232.

[144] Saint Athanasius, *On the Incarnation* (Crestwood, NY: St. Vladimir's Seminary Press, 1996), 41.

[145] Romans 8:22 NASB.

[146] John 1:14 NKJV.

By becoming one of us, Jesus makes it possible for our bodies to be deified along with our souls. This is why we venerate the saints and reverence their icons and relics. The bodies of the saints are transfigured by the divine light of the Transfiguration.[147]

Deification begins in the present.[148] Jesus offers the abundant life[149] to us, and our life in Christ begins now. Although we are "dead to sin but alive to God in Christ Jesus,"[150] we still may sin and continually need to repent.[151] The Jesus Prayer invites us to "pray without ceasing,"[152] recognizing Jesus as Lord, Messiah, and Son of God. We beg for mercy and acknowledge our sin. We visit the Sacrament of Confession to get right with God. Our repentance allows the process of deification to continue within the simple and ordinary acts of our Christian life: Church, Sacrament, Scripture, prayer, and obedience to God's commandments.[153] God calls us to love and serve.

Every Wednesday, all day long in the middle of our workweek, we can begin to anticipate our celebration of the Divine Liturgy on Sunday by embracing the Virtue of Holiness. Here is one small example. We can recall how just a few days earlier at Mass, we received the Body and

---

[147] Ware, *Orthodox Church*, 233.//
[148] Ibid., 236.
[149] John 10:10b.
[150] Romans 6:11 NIV.
[151] Ware, *Orthodox Church*, 236.
[152] 1 Thessalonians 5:17 NASB.
[153] Ware, *Orthodox Church*, 236.

Blood of Christ, perhaps the surest path to holiness. Being Orthodox is experiential, and reflecting each hump day how the Body and Blood of Christ in the Eucharist enriches our lives as we advance towards God in our ongoing quest for holiness.

CHAPTER FOUR

THURSDAY

THE VIRTUE OF LOVE

Jesus answered him, "The first of all the commandments is: 'Hear, O Israel, the Lord our God, the Lord is one. And you shall love the Lord your God with all your heart, with all your soul, with all your mind, and with all your strength.' This is the first commandment. And the second, like it, is this: 'You shall love your neighbor as yourself.' There is no other commandment greater than these" (Mark 12:29-31 NKJV).

The most popular day of the workweek is Friday, but Thursday is a close second. On the eve of "Happy Friday," Thursday is just a couple steps away from a fun weekend. This is the perfect day to focus on the Virtue of Love. "And we have known and believed the love that God has for us. God is love, and he who abides in love abides in God, and God in him."[154]

---

[154] 1 John 4:16 NKJV.

Dad was my hero and friend, the best Dad in the world. Dad fought with honour and valor at Guadalcanal in the Second World War. He told me once about what almost became a memorable misadventure. He said they were fighting the Japanese on a beach. As he and his troops ran forward, machine gun bullets sprayed the sand right in front of him, and he and his men scurried back for cover. On an unrelated note, Mom recalls how Dad and his Army friends made hooch with a still and drank the harshest of wartime liquor.

Dad also carried a beautiful wooden-carved chess set with him everywhere, as chess is an international game, and he always could find players while travelling to different destinations at home and abroad. As the faculty leader of Cardinal Chess at school, I enjoyed using Dad's magnificent chess set to battle Joseph, our scholarly undefeated student champion, during the school-wide Christmas party one year.

An Army buddy got a job for Dad at Marshall Field's in downtown Chicago, and Mom was one of the working girls eyeing this new Army officer once he arrived. Dad was thirty-nine and Mom was twenty-seven when they got married at Fort Sheridan outside Chicago on New Year's Eve a few years after the war. Six months after the birth of his first son, Dad led men from two Illinois National Guard units to maintain order after a riot erupted in a Chicago suburb after mobs destroyed a house into which a Black man and his family attempted to move. Colonel Lochbihler was quoted as saying the strength of the National Guard units he commanded "is of sufficient size to handle the situation."[155]

I was the youngest of four children, all of us two years apart, and Dad was already forty-eight years old when I was born. Dad came home from work one day with baseball cards for my brother Vince and me, and I remember my first baseball card ever, a Topps 1966 Willie Mays. Beginning in about fourth grade and extending through my first two years of high school, Dad and I shared countless adventures together each Saturday morning in Fort Wayne, and our regular routine was classic fun. Dad sold insurance, and we began some Saturday mornings at his office, with him catching up on paperwork while I calculated baseball statistics from our card and board game seasons, both batting averages with long division and pitching earned run averages with a slide rule. We then drove to Allen County Public Library, with a giant globe of the earth inside, and I scurried to the sports book section to read about my heroes in baseball, football, and basketball. Next was an occasional stop at Arnold Palmer Dry Cleaning if Dad had some business shirts to drop off or pick up. Dad and I visited Fort Wayne's first indoor mall, Glenbrook Square, and nearby Northcrest Shopping Center before settling down for a sirloin at Ponderosa Steak House or a burger at Big Boy Restaurant.

Dad gave the best gift of all to me, his time, and my childhood was abundantly blessed because of his love and presence. Besides being my best friend, Dad was also my

---

[155] "Local Guardsmen at Riot Scene: Berwyn Outfits Relieve 44th Division Units; All Quiet in Disorder Area," *The Berwyn Life*, July 18, 1951, p. 1.

hero. I told him this after graduating from the University of Texas School of Law as we were saying goodbye. Cancer struck Dad very hard a year later, and several months later I sat with him, holding his hand and praying the Rosary, the moment he died.

Dad had slipped into a comatose state a few days earlier, when suddenly, the day before he died, Dad emerged from being glassy-eyed, looking around and appearing lucid. As I stood there in front of Dad, Mom asked him, "Do you see David?" Dad shook his head no. Mom then asked, "Do you see Jesus?" Dad nodded yes! Within minutes he slipped back into his unresponsive, unaware state.

As I prayed the Rosary by Dad the next day, holding his hand, his breathing began to slow. He stopped breathing as I continued saying the Hail Marys, and after less than a minute, his lungs emitted one or two final heavy, deep breaths. I continued holding Dad's hand, praying the Rosary, before the face of death. I lost my best friend, my hero, my Dad; life would never be the same. Nearly four decades later, it seems like I remember him most every day. The Virtue of Love comes readily to my heart each time I think about Dad, turning my thoughts to how we as Orthodox Christians live the Great Commandment in our lives with our beloved families each day.

As we strive towards holiness, deification is a social not a solitary process grounded in the Great Commandment.[156] "God is love,"[157] and Jesus the only-begotten Son of God calls

---

[156] Ware, *Orthodox Church*, 237.
[157] 1 John 4:16 NKJV.

us to love God and love our neighbor.[158] Although other religions call us to love, Christianity offers the best way for this to occur. "The newness of Christianity lies not in the commandment to love, but in the fact that it has become possible to fulfil the commandment."[159] We live in Christ through the power of the indwelling Holy Spirit, and in doing so, we seek to experience uncreated grace in our union and communion with God through the process of deification. Only by living in Christ and with the power of the Holy Spirit, active within the Church and immersed in the Sacraments, are we truly and abundantly able to begin to love God and love our neighbor.

Yet Jesus calls us further and deeper. "But I say unto you, Love your enemies, bless them that curse you, do good to them that hate you, and pray for them which despitefully use you, and persecute you."[160] The Torah calls us to love God[161] and love our neighbor.[162] As we strive in Christ for union and communion with God, we are challenged to love not only God and neighbor but our enemies as well. Jesus calls us to feed the hungry, give drink to the thirsty, offer hospitality to the stranger, clothe the naked, and visit the sick and the prisoners.[163] Saint Antony the Great of Egypt declared, "If it were possible for me to

---

[158] Matthew 22:37-39.

[159] Alexander Schmemann, *The Eucharist* (Crestwood, NY: St. Vladimir's Seminary Press, 1987), 136.

[160] Matthew 5:44 KJV.

[161] Deuteronomy 6:5.

[162] Leviticus 19:18.

[163] Matthew 25:35-36.

find a leper and to give him my body and to take his, I would do it. For this is perfect love."[164] Difficult as these challenges may seem, with God all things are possible.[165]

During a Wednesday Family Night youth group meeting at Saint Patrick Orthodox Church several years ago, I taught a lesson about Philippians 2:5-11. Specifically, Jesus "in the form of God" took "the form of a bondservant" and came "in appearance as a man."[166] We studied the New Testament Greek, and the students learned that although Jesus' *schema* was that of a man, His *morphe* included His identity as both God and bondservant. In other words, Jesus' *schema*, what men saw on the outside, revealed only a man, but his *morphe*, who He was deep down inside, included His identity as both God and bondservant.

Truly "the basis of pastoral theology rests in the theological dynamic of the incarnation."[167] Just as Jesus was fully God and fully man, we live "more abundantly"[168] by receiving the Body and Blood of Christ during the Divine Liturgy. "I believe and I confess that for the Church, for the world, for mankind there is no more important, more urgent question than *what is accomplished in the eucharist*."[169] This is especially true when our young people not only receive the Eucharist but also allow it to permeate their whole being and actually define their *morphe*, who

---

[164] Ware, *Orthodox Church*, 237.
[165] Matthew 19:26.
[166] Philippians 2:6-8 NKJV.
[167] Allen, *Orthodox Synthesis*, 104.
[168] John 10:10 KJV.
[169] Schmemann, *The Eucharist*, 163 (emphasis in original).

they are deep down inside: "He that eateth my flesh, and drinketh my blood, dwelleth in me, and I in him."[170] After experiencing the Eucharist as what Father Alexander Schmemann called "an ascension to heaven, our entrance into the heavenly sanctuary,"[171] our youth group through their community service brought the light of Christ into "a deeper solidarity with the poor, the hungry, the sick, the dying, and the oppressed."[172]

"My belief is that we best grasp the meaning of the incarnation when we *experience* the truth that in Christ, God placed Himself in the world, even sharing and experiencing the debasement of the human condition, and ultimately the final humiliation: death."[173] Within the Orthodox Church, our theology calls us to be like Christ, to freely love and serve, "Thy Kingdom come, Thy will be done in earth, as it is in heaven."[174] We are called to "not be conformed to this world, but be transformed by the renewing of your mind, that you may prove what the will of God is, that which is good and acceptable and perfect."[175] The incarnation is lived out in our pastoral theology if we like Saint Irenaeus realize, "The glory of God is man most fully alive, and the life of man is the vision of God."[176]

---

[170] John 6:56 KJV.
[171] Allen, *Orthodox Synthesis*, 44.
[172] Nouwen et al, *Compassion*, 117.
[173] Allen, *Orthodox Synthesis*, 104 (emphasis in original).
[174] Matthew 6:10 KJV.
[175] Romans 12:2 NASB.
[176] Allen, *Orthodox Synthesis*, 104.

Truly we need to heed the words of Saint Paul: "Let this mind be in you which was also in Christ Jesus."[177] We are to follow in the footprints of Christ. "Jesus is the obedient servant who hears the call and desires to respond even when it leads him to pain and suffering. This desire is not to experience pain, but to give his full undivided attention to the voice of his beloved Father."[178] Our Orthodox theology defines and gives depth to our pastoral ministry when we seek to do the same. "In prayer we meet Christ, and in him all human suffering. In service we meet people, and in them the suffering Christ."[179] Within this Orthodox paradigm, theology and pastoral ministry merge.

Both Baptism and the Eucharist invite us to "pass over" into the Kingdom of God. As the water of Baptism is holy through the presence of Christ and the Holy Spirit, the bread and wine in the Eucharist are truly "the Body and Blood of Christ, His *parousia*, His presence among us."[180] As a result, the gates are open for our union and communion with God. The sacraments of Baptism and Eucharist are means to the end, the end being our deification in Christ, knowledge of and communion with God.[181]

"In the beginning was the Word, and the Word was with God, and the Word was God."[182] According to Professor Vladimir Lossky, "He Who is incarnated is indeed

---

[177] Philippians 2:5 NKJV.
[178] Nouwen et al, *Compassion*, 39.
[179] Ibid., 117.
[180] Schmemann, *Of Water & Spirit*, 50.
[181] Ibid., 50.
[182] John 1:1 NKJV.

none other than the Word, that is to say, the second person of the Trinity. Incarnation and Trinity are thus inseparable."[183] The evangelist Saint John in declaring "the Word was made flesh, and dwelt among us"[184] presented Jesus the Son of God as the second person in the Trinity. Because the Word was with God, a relationship exists between the Father and the Son. Because the Word was God, this relationship involves the fullness of divinity. This "relationship between the Father and the Son is eternal generation, and we are thus introduced, by the Gospel itself, to the life of the divine persons of the Trinity."[185] Saint John the Theologian, in recording the Last Supper discourse, introduces through the teaching of Jesus the third person of the Trinity, the Holy Spirit. "And I will pray the Father, and he shall give you another Comforter, that he may abide with you for ever: *Even* the Spirit of truth."[186] Jesus later tells His disciples, "But the Comforter, *which is* the Holy Ghost, whom the Father will send in my name, he shall teach you all things, and bring all things to your remembrance, whatsoever I have said unto you."[187]

"The Son and the Spirit thus appear, throughout the Gospel, as two divine persons sent into the world, the former to quicken our personal liberty, the latter to unite

---

[183] Vladimir Lossky, *Orthodox Theology: An Introduction*, translated by Ian and Ihita Kesarcodi-Watson (Crestwood, NY: St. Vladimir's Seminary Press, 1978), 36.

[184] John 1:14 KJV.

[185] Lossky, *Orthodox Theology: An Introduction*, 38.

[186] John 14:16-17a KJV.

[187] John 14:26 KJV.

Itself to our nature and regenerate it."[188] The Son and the Spirit readily are distinguished in two respects. First, their relationship with God the Father differs in kind. Whereas Jesus is the "only begotten Son"[189] of the Father, the Holy Spirit "proceedeth from the Father."[190] Second, the Son and the Spirit relate uniquely to each other. Whereas "it is thanks to the purification of the Virgin by the Spirit that the Son could be given to men, as it is by the prayer of the Son ascended back to the right hand of the Father that the Spirit is dispensed to them."[191] Both God the Son and God the Holy Spirit are "equal in dignity to the Father and identical to Him in substance."[192]

Because we are dealing with the ultimate mystery in discussing the Holy Trinity, a rational or dialectical approach to understanding is doomed to fail. The goal of apophatic theology is to prayerfully experience rather than logically understand the infinite. In the silence of contemplation, human reason is stilled, the imagination is quieted, and prayer occurs with neither preconception nor passion. "Here wordless, contemplative prayer begins; the prayer in which the heart lays itself open in silence before God."[193] Although we cannot know God in His essence, we can perceive Him in His energies. "To see God is to contemplate the Trinity while fully participating in

---

[188] Lossky, *Orthodox Theology: An Introduction*, 39.
[189] John 3:16 KJV.
[190] John 15:26 KJV.
[191] Lossky, *Orthodox Theology: An Introduction*, 39.
[192] Ibid.
[193] Lossky, *The Mystical Theology of the Eastern Church*, 206.

His light."[194] As we ponder the Trinity in prayer, we strive to embrace the God of love. "The fruit of prayer is divine love, which is simply grace, appropriated in the depth of our being."[195]

The fourth century proved pivotal in our Orthodox contemplative appreciation of the Trinity. Although Saint Athanasius did not directly describe the Holy Spirit as God, "his doctrine is that He belongs to the Word and the Father, and shares one and the same substance (ὁμοούσιος) with Them."[196] Similarly, Saint Basil the Great "nowhere calls the Spirit God or affirms His consubstantiality in so many words, although he makes it plain that 'we glorify the Spirit with the Father and the Son because we believe that He is not alien to the divine nature.'"[197] Saint Gregory Nazianzen, on the other hand, declares the Holy Spirit to be both God and consubstantial with the Father and the Son.[198] Specifically, "as the Father so the Son, as the Son so the Holy Ghost; the Three, one God when contemplated together; each God because consubstantial; the Three, one God because of the monarchy."[199] Finally, Gregory of Nyssa distinguishes between the three persons of the Trinity in a furtherance of theological thought: "The Spirit, he

---

[194] Vladimir Lossky, *The Vision of God* (Crestwood, New York: St. Vladimir's Seminary Press, 1963), 81.

[195] Lossky, *The Mystical Theology of the Eastern Church*, 212.

[196] J.N.D. Kelly, *Early Christian Doctrines*, rev. ed. (New York: HarperOne, 1978), 258.

[197] Ibid., 260-261.

[198] Ibid., 261.

[199] Lossky, *The Mystical Theology of the Eastern Church*, 63.

teaches, is out of God and is of Christ; He proceeds out of the Father and receives from the Son; He cannot be separated from the Word."[200]

The fourth-century Cappadocian fathers were concerned more with salvation rather than speculation about the Triune God.[201] The Nicene Creed professed the divinity of God the Father, God the Son, and God the Holy Spirit. Specifically, "the incarnate Logos and the Holy Spirit are met and experienced first as *divine agents of salvation*, and only then are they also discovered to be essentially one God."[202] "The Nicaean doctrine of consubstantiality meant 'the confession of the fullness of divinity in Christ and implied that the Incarnation was essential to the redemptive act of Christ'; and maintained, similarly, that if 'the Spirit is not fully God, He is unable to bestow sanctification.'"[203]

The consubstantiality of both the Son and the Spirit was "formally endorsed"[204] at the Council of Constantinople in 381. For the Cappadocians, God the Father is "the source, fountain-head or principle of the Godhead."[205] Yet the Cappadocian Fathers did not stop there. Going beyond Saint Athanasius, the Cappadocians "were em-

---

[200] Kelly, *Early Christian Doctrines*, 262.

[201] John Meyendorff, *Byzantine Theology: Historical Trends and Doctrinal Themes* (Crestwood, NY: St. Vladimir's Seminary Press, 1980), 180.

[202] Ibid.

[203] Ibid.

[204] Kelly, *Early Christian Doctrines*, 263.

[205] Ibid., 265.

phatic that the three hypostases share one and the same nature. In the Triad the Monad is adored, just as the Triad is adored in the Monad; and the distinction of hypostases in no way renders the oneness of nature asunder."[206] Stated another way, "The Church has expressed by the *ὁμοούσιος* the consubstantiality of the Three, the mysterious identity of the monad and of the triad; identity of the one nature and distinction of the three hypostases."[207] Although the Father, Son, and Holy Spirit are three distinct persons, their essence is identical. "Thus if Father, Son and Spirit are distinguishable numerically as Persons, They are indistinguishable as essence."[208]

"The Greek Fathers always maintained that the principle of unity in the Trinity is the person of the Father."[209] According to Saint Maximus the Confessor in the seventh century, God the Father distinguishes the hypostases in the Trinity "in an eternal movement of love."[210] In other words, God the Father "confers His one nature upon the Son and upon the Holy Spirit alike, in whom it remains one and undivided, not distributed, while being differently conferred; for the procession of the Holy Spirit from the Father is not identical with the generation of the Son by the same Father."[211]

---

[206] Ibid., 266.
[207] Lossky, *The Mystical Theology of the Eastern Church*, 48-49.
[208] Kelly, *Early Christian Doctrines*, 268.
[209] Lossky, *The Mystical Theology of the Eastern Church*, 58.
[210] Ibid., 60.
[211] Ibid.

Just as Saint Athanasius and the Cappadocian Fathers provided critical teaching about the Trinity in the East, Saint Augustine "gave the Western tradition its mature and final expression."[212]

Unlike in the East, whose theologians made God the Father the essential starting point for understanding the Trinity, Saint Augustine began with the divine nature of the Trinity.[213] According to this Western perspective, "each of the divine Persons, from the point of view of substance, is identical with the others or with the divine substance itself."[214] Because "the Trinity possesses a single, indivisible action and a single will," there is no difference in either natures or wills.[215] Saint John Damascene in the eighth century described how the three persons of the Holy Trinity have "but one nature, have but a single will, a single power, a single operation."[216]

God the Son and God the Spirit coexist with God the Father in the Holy Trinity. "They transcend the world where they act: the one and the other indeed are 'with' the Father, Who does not Himself come into the world, and their closeness to the Father, source of the divine nature, manages to locate for our thought the Trinity in its transcendence, its stability and its fullness."[217] We joyfully contemplate the essence of the Triune God without

---

[212] Kelly, *Early Christian Doctrines*, 271.

[213] Ibid., 272.

[214] Ibid., 272-273.

[215] Ibid., 273.

[216] Lossky, *The Mystical Theology of the Eastern Church*, 53.

[217] Lossky, *Orthodox Theology: An Introduction*, 39.

any dialectical development. "The triumph of Christian thought is to have elaborated over the first four centuries, and particularly during the fourth, 'trinitarian' *par excellence*, a definition which gives to the heathen an inkling of the fullness of the Trinity: this was not the rationalization of Christianity but the Christianization of reason, a transmuting of philosophy into contemplation, a saturation of thought by a mystery which is not a secret to conceal, but an inexhaustible light."[218] The Trinity infinitely exemplifies love. "He is triunity: three equal persons, each one dwelling in the other two by virtue of an unceasing movement of mutual love."[219]

Throughout the day every Thursday, we are called to take some time to focus on the Virtue of Love. "God is love, and the one who abides in love abides in God, and God abides in him."[220] The eternal love of the Holy Trinity calls us to embrace the Virtue of Love. As Orthodox Christians immersed in an ongoing love relationship with God in Christ, the power and presence of the Holy Spirit in our lives frees us to love our neighbor and empowers us to forgive and even love our enemies.[221]

---

[218] Ibid., 38.

[219] Kallistos Ware, *The Orthodox Way* (Crestwood, New York: St. Vladimir's Seminary Press, 1979), 14.

[220] 1 John 4:16b NASB.

[221] Matthew 5:43-44.

CHAPTER FIVE

FRIDAY

THE VIRTUE OF LONGSUFFERING

He was despised and forsaken of men,
A man of sorrows and acquainted with grief;
And like one from whom men hide their face
He was despised, and we did not esteem Him.

Surely our griefs He Himself bore,
And our sorrows He carried;
Yet we ourselves esteemed Him stricken,
Smitten of God, and afflicted.

But He was pierced through for our transgressions,
He was crushed for our iniquities;
The chastening for our well-being *fell* upon Him,
And by His scourging we are healed
(Isaiah 53:3-5 NASB).

What the New American Standard Bible calls "patience" in Galatians 5:22, the King James Version translates as "longsuffering." We celebrate the end of the workweek by wishing each other a "Happy Friday." As Orthodox

Christians, we fast and abstain each Friday among other days while recalling our Lord's crucifixion and death. The Virtue of Longsuffering directs us towards the Cross of Christ.

After the academic rigor of each of the three years at the University of Texas School of Law, we were given the opportunity to apply for and serve as summer law clerks in a variety of situations and locations. Going to a top law firm, you could earn a great summer salary and land on their radar for a possible future lucrative offer. I decided after my first year to travel in a different direction by serving with Legal Services Corporation as a summer law clerk on the Navajo Nation in Chinle, Arizona. Besides engaging in some memorable legal experiences, I biked often to view natural wonders in the Canyon de Chelly and hiked to the bottom of the Grand Canyon twice.

During my second summer in law school, I decided to go the more traditional route by clerking at a prestigious downtown Chicago law firm. That summer I travelled to Marquette University to hear Mother Teresa of Calcutta speak. Her speech, nearly a decade after the infamous 1973 *Roe v. Wade* Supreme Court decision legalizing abortion in the United States, pointed to the sinfulness of this new immoral yet legal reality. With her soft voice but without mincing words, Mother Teresa spoke eloquently about the scourge of abortion in America. She wondered why anyone could doubt the sanctity of life by referring to the powerful presence of Jesus in Mary's womb when Our Lady visited her cousin Elizabeth. "And whence is this to me, that the mother of my Lord should come to me? For, lo, as soon as the voice of thy salutation sounded in mine ears, the babe leaped in my womb for joy."[222] Surely the emerging life in the womb is both human and sacred. The recent landmark Supreme Court decision *Dobbs v. Jackson Women's Health Organization* overruled *Roe v. Wade* after nearly half a century.

These two summer experiences proved to be pivotal events in my life. With the Navajo people, besides my summer legal clerkship, I served as a volunteer at both a home for exceptional children and a nursing home, Chinle being the site of the only two such homes within the entire Navajo Nation four decades ago. The home for exceptional children cared for students with learning disabilities. This unique adventure reminded me of my senior year at Notre Dame when I visited the Logan Center just off campus, a similar facility, and served two Down's Syndrome children, feeding Mikel in his wheelchair and taking Philip to the circus.

Many Navajos at the time lived in mud huts called hogans and lacked the luxury of electricity and running water. At the nursing home, I saw one elderly man rinse his hands in the toilet, looking undoubtedly by him like a source of clean and fresh water. Another resident in his early twenties lived at the home after losing both his legs after an alcohol-related traffic accident. These two Navajo men spanning two generations seemed destined to spend their remaining days and years in this nursing home.

---

[222] Luke 1:43-44 KJV.

The life of the Blessed Virgin Mary best exemplifies the Virtue of Longsuffering experienced by the Theotokos as she courageously faced the crushing blows of painful sorrow. The Roman authorities convicted as a criminal and condemned to die by tortuous crucifixion the Holy Child she nursed as a baby, the Holy Child she consoled when He cried as a boy, the Holy Child she loved and nurtured into manhood and mission. As Mary followed Jesus to Calvary and stood at the foot of His Cross, she suffered more than any other human being in the history of the world.

The prophet Simeon held the Holy Child and told His Mother "a sword shall pierce through thine own soul."[223] A mother's love for her son knows no bounds, and she will do anything to take his suffering upon herself. No pain was more exquisite, yet Mary the Theotokos endured the Cross of her Son with joyful sorrow. "Now I rejoice in my sufferings for your sake, and in my flesh I do my share on behalf of His body, which is the church, in filling up what is lacking in Christ's afflictions."[224]

Both the life of Mary and my own summer experiences epitomized the longsuffering inherent in the Cross of Christ. There is great sadness in suffering, but with this sorrow comes the joyful anticipation of resurrection and new life.

"Jesus the Logos has two *natures* or *essences*, consubstantial with both the Father and with us."[225] As divine,

---

[223] Luke 2:35a ERV.

[224] Colossians 1:24 NASB.

[225] Brian Donohue, Email to David Lochbihler, 23 December 2021 (emphasis in original).

He was the "Son of God"; as man, "He was born from the Virgin."[226] Tertullian's description of the Incarnation is profound: "He entered into the Virgin, as the angel of the annunciation foretold, and received His flesh from her."[227] Although Mary conceived as a virgin, she never lost her virginity as Jesus was born from and not through her.[228] Specifically, "Christ's humanity was in every respect genuine, and also complete; it included, as indispensable to man's constitution, a soul as well as a body – indeed, the assumption of a soul was necessary if man was to be saved."[229] Jesus had to become fully man in the Incarnation, from conception to the Cross, were the entirety of man to be redeemed. Jesus was fully human and experienced "hunger and thirst, tears, birth and death."[230] Yet He also was fully God, as the Word was His "governing principle in His make-up," and that "it was he, the divine spirit, Who 'took the man to Himself' … and 'mingled God and man in Himself.'"[231]

This mingling together lies at the heart of Christology. How do the two natures or essences of Christ commingle? "Tertullian has the distinction of being the first theologian frankly to tackle this issue."[232] To address this complexity, Tertullian offered two alternatives: " 'Thus the Word is

---

[226] Kelly, *Early Christian Doctrines*, 150.
[227] Ibid.
[228] Ibid.
[229] Ibid., 150-151.
[230] Ibid., 151.
[231] Ibid.
[232] Ibid.

in flesh. But this provokes the inquiry how the Word became flesh. Was He, so to speak, metamorphosed … into flesh, or did He clothe Himself in it'?"[233] Because God is immutable and unchanging, Tertullian chose the latter option. "The logical conclusion is that both 'substances' continue unaltered and unimpaired after the union" as "each of them preserves its peculiar qualities."[234] From his perspective, Tertullian saw "the spirit performing the miracles and the humanity enduring the sufferings."[235] Most pertinent for future Christological developments, "He Who was both Son of God and Son of man was one and the same Person."[236] Tertullian "sums up: 'We observe a twofold condition, not confused but conjoined, Jesus, in one Person at once God and man.'"[237]

Jesus suffered and died on the Cross, and through His Resurrection we are offered new life in Christ. "Therefore we have been buried with Him through baptism into death, so that as Christ was raised from the dead through the glory of the Father, so we too might walk in newness of life."[238] With these words, Saint Paul describes the heart of Baptism, our dying with Christ and our death to sin, and our resurrection with Christ into new life, "dead indeed to sin, but alive to God in Christ Jesus our Lord."[239]

---

[233] Ibid.
[234] Ibid.
[235] Ibid.
[236] Ibid.
[237] Ibid.
[238] Romans 6:4 NASB.
[239] Romans 6:11 NKJV.

Filled with the power and presence of the Holy Spirit, we are free to choose not to sin.

As surely as darkness precedes the dawn, the scourge of sin desperately needs repentance and redemption in Christ. Saint Antony the Great battled demons and advised others on how to defeat them because " 'they are nothing and they disappear quickly–especially if one fortifies himself with faith and the sign of the cross.'"[240] Although Saint Antony urged the monks from necessity to focus only a little on the body, the body would be subservient to the soul to such an extent their devotion to the soul would be maximized.[241] By remembering death as an essential part of life, Saint Antony encouraged the monks, " 'For if we so live as people dying daily, we will not commit sin.'"[242]

Friday is the perfect day to focus on longsuffering most visible in the Cross of Christ. Like the Virgin Mary, we too may stand at the foot of the Cross of Christ and see her beloved Son bleed, suffer, and die. We all bleed, we all suffer, and we will all die. Yet with the Theotokos our sorrow may turn into joy if we strive to live and not seek to escape or deny our own suffering. By welcoming the Virtue of Longsuffering, we walk with Mary in understanding that "unless a grain of wheat falls into the ground and dies, it remains alone; but if it dies, it produces much grain."[243]

---

[240] Saint Athanasius, *The Life of Antony and the Letter to Marcellinus*, 48.

[241] Ibid., 65.

[242] Ibid., 45.

[243] John 12:24 NKJV.

CHAPTER SIX

SATURDAY

THE VIRTUE OF PRAYER

> Be anxious for nothing, but in everything by prayer
> and supplication with thanksgiving let your requests
> be made known to God. And the peace of God,
> which surpasses all comprehension, will guard
> your hearts and your minds in Christ Jesus
> (Philippians 4:6-7 NASB).

The many tasks of a busy workweek finally accomplished, we may sleep in and relax a bit, enjoying the weekend and our time at home with family and at church with friends. Saturday also is the perfect time to step back and embrace the Virtue of Prayer. After briefly reflecting upon the gains and losses of this past week, we can experience with joy a day off work while anticipating our visits to church for both Vespers that evening and Matins and Mass, the Divine Liturgy, in the morning.

Saint Charles Borromeo Church added magnificent beauty to my childhood. My family could go to Mass at a variety of times each Sunday, and we usually went at either

9:30 or 11:00 in the morning. One time we had the bright idea of going to the earliest Mass at 6:30 in the morning in order to enjoy so much more of a full morning and a long afternoon at home. The plan sounded good on paper, but all I remember is driving back from Mass, excited at all the free time ahead of us, yet our whole family felt exhausted by early afternoon and needed to take an afternoon nap.

There was a big fire at Saint Charles during our grade school years, and the charred, black Cross remains behind glass in a hallway today as a beautiful relic and remembrance of my pure and holy childhood faith. Life was simple, and we played baseball, football, and basketball, both inside and outside. Our faith was real and brought great joy and stability to our lives. Our Liturgy was rich, our church was filled with gold and glitter, and our hearts were encouraged to stay pure and to live holy lives for Jesus and Mary.

After sixth and seventh grades, in the summer, I went for a week to a Roman Catholic seminary camp for boys in Holland, Michigan. Mom and Dad dropped me off, and I remember, because it was my first time away from home, being very homesick. The seminarians were great, and it was a very positive experience. We asked one of them what he thought of English class, thinking he would give a holy and positive response. All he said was, "English stinks." The priests told the corniest jokes, two punch lines being "Come to me, my melon collie baby" and "I wouldn't send a knight out on a dog like this." We had fun playing softball (I was the first baseman), and the day ended with "The Grand Silence." One night we were talking so loudly and goofing around after lights out, the whole dorm was pulled out of bed and had to run laps in the gym. I remember being called out of class once, and the priest spoke to me in the hallway about my vocation to the priesthood and had very positive and encouraging words to say.

I saw the Virtue of Prayer displayed each day in the life of my elderly grandmother. Grandma lived to be 103, praying the Rosary faithfully as long as her mind allowed, every single day, twice a day. When she was a little girl, my Mom was once very sick. Grandma promised to pray the Rosary every day if her daughter recovered. Mom recovered, and Grandma faithfully kept this promise. Later in life, when one of my brothers was rushed to the hospital during an asthma attack, Grandma again promised to say a second Rosary if he recovered. Her prayer request granted, Grandma honoured her commitment and began praying two Rosaries every day. During my Christmas breaks from Notre Dame, Grandma and I often talked late into the night. To ensure she kept her prayer commitment, Grandma would begin to say her Rosaries right at the stroke of midnight to fulfill that day's dual obligation just prior to going to sleep.

Archbishop Bloom tells a similar story about a 102-year-old woman understanding the relevance of silence within a life of prayer. She discovered "this silence was not simply an absence of noise, but that the silence had substance. It was not the absence of something but presence of something. The silence had a density, a richness, and it began to pervade me. The silence around began to come and meet the silence in me."[244] A deep and abiding love for Jesus, Our Lady, and the saints needs to permeate our prayer life all day long. How often do our prayers intended for God turn into a narrow thinking about our problems and a mere talking to ourselves? In the presence of God, we need to take time to simply listen and love. The simple yet powerful prayer of listening and loving begins and ends in silence.

Each Saturday we focus on the Virtue of Prayer, taking time throughout the day not only to pray but also to visualize how the many moments of our lives we offer and dedicate to God are daily expressions of prayer. Prayer and love are inexorably linked together as one. "The knowledge of God through prayer and love for Him are closely bound together."[245] Jesus described the Great Commandment as our love for God and neighbor.[246] We partake in the divine nature to the extent our prayer expresses a deep and abiding love for God. "The fruit of prayer is divine love."[247] Yet our love for God is linked by Jesus with our love for our neighbor. Father Maximos expresses this inevitable connection between our love for God and our love for our neighbor superbly: "If you learn to love God through prayer then it is natural to love your neighbor. In fact it is inevitable since the two go together."[248]

---

[244] Bloom, *Beginning to Pray*, 93.
[245] Stavropouplos, *Partakers of Divine Nature*, 72.
[246] Luke 10:27.
[247] Stavropouplos, *Partakers of Divine Nature*, 79.
[248] Markides, *Gifts of the Desert*, 209.

Prayer is so much more than words. "Every sacred movement of the heart, every pure emotion, every thought of God, every activity of the mind and heart done in the spirit of God, every spiritual elevation and every spiritual activity, as well as all spiritual study, are included in the word 'prayer.'"[249] Purity of heart lies at the heart of prayer. "A characteristic condition of true Christian prayer is purity."[250] This purity of the heart clears away all our transitory imaginings. "It is absolutely necessary for our mind to be wiped clean of every external image and idea."[251] We pray as best as we are able, but with God's grace the prayer within the deepest recesses of our hearts shifts from what we try to do to what God does in us. "There is a moment when the Holy Spirit changes rational prayer into noetic prayer: He turns the prayer we are saying with our reason into words uttered by the noetic faculty."[252] Buoyed by this experience, the saints did not just pray, but their lives become a prayer. "The whole life of a saint is one great prayer."[253] The Apostle Paul calls and challenges us to "pray without ceasing."[254] What does this mean? "Unceasing prayer is nothing other than a constant and living communion of human beings with God."[255]

---

[249] Stavropouplos, *Partakers of Divine Nature*, 66-67.

[250] Ibid., 70.

[251] Ibid., 74.

[252] Hierotheos, *Hesychia and Theology: The Context for Man's Healing in the Orthodox Church*, 164.

[253] Stavropouplos, *Partakers of Divine Nature*, 67.

[254] 1 Thessalonians 5:17 NASB.

[255] Stavropouplos, *Partakers of Divine Nature*, 79.

"The day when God is absent, when He is silent – that is the beginning of prayer."[256] I love Jesus and Mary and the saints, I yearn for the Eucharist, I try despite my inherent selfishness to love both neighbor and enemies. Prayer leads to a depth in one's heart, and "the Christian is like someone who lives in three dimensions in a world in which the majority of people live in two."[257] How often are our feeble efforts at prayer at worst one-dimensional (we talk to ourselves) and at best two-dimensional (trying to talk to God but not listening)? Once with God's grace our prayer becomes three-dimensional (trying to listen to God), we still will fall infinitely short of God living in a reality far beyond the fourth dimension (the place of loving God). Because God is so indescribably immense, we can expect to be "beginning to pray" our whole life long.

The Eastern Orthodox Church faithful pray each Sunday, "thou art God ineffable, inconceivable, invisible, incomprehensible, ever-existing and eternally the same, thou and thine only-begotten Son and thy Holy Spirit."[258] With these words at the start of the Holy Anaphora during the Divine Liturgy of Saint John Chrysostom, we proclaim the utter transcendence and unknowability of the Trinity. Compared to our infinite and uncreated God, man is finite and created, as expressed in the next line from the Holy Anaphora: "Thou it was who didst bring us from

---

[256] Bloom, *Beginning to Pray*, 17.
[257] Ibid., 18.
[258] *The Divine and Holy Liturgy of the Orthodox Church* (Louisville, KY: St. Michael the Archangel Orthodox Church, 2007), 41.

non-existence into being."[259] Our inward purification and genuine contemplation lead to union and communion with God.

Our ultimate purpose in life is union and communion with God. "For Ignatius, with his intense Christ-mysticism, the essence of salvation seems to consist in union with Christ, through whom new life and immortality flow into us. He dwells in us, so that we become His temple."[260] According to Saint Ignatius, "Because of His measureless love, He became what we are in order to enable us to become what He is."[261] Our primary purpose is not to learn more about God but rather to become more like God: "He, indeed, assumed humanity that we might become God."[262] With these words, Saint Athanasius describes the doctrine of deification or *theosis*, the heart and deepest endeavor of Orthodoxy.

"Salvation is ... communion and union with Christ, and, through Him, with the Holy Trinity, since the energy of the Triune God is common."[263] This Trinitarian truth permeates apophatic theology. "The whole vision of God will be trinitarian: a vision in the Holy Spirit, through the Son, directed toward the Father."[264] According to Saint John Chrysostom, God goes out of His own nature and

---

[259] Ibid.

[260] Kelly, *Early Christian Doctrines*, 164.

[261] Ibid., 172.

[262] Saint Athanasius, *On the Incarnation*, 93.

[263] Hierotheos, *The Illness and Cure of the Soul in the Orthodox Theology*, 105.

[264] Lossky, *The Vision of God*, 81.

descends to His creatures through the Incarnation.[265] In fact, "the Incarnation of the Word has no other goal than to lead us to the Father, in the Spirit."[266] God speaks to us through His Son, through the Incarnation. "Every energy, every manifestation, comes from the Father, is expressed in the Son, and goes forth in the Holy Spirit."[267]

"Blessed are the pure in heart, for they shall see God."[268] Within the Orthodox Church, mystery and dogma merge together as we strive in prayer to draw closer to Almighty God with a pure heart. "The eastern tradition has never made a sharp distinction between mysticism and theology; between personal experience of the divine mysteries and the dogma affirmed by the Church."[269] The shift from positive to negative theology changes us from the inside-out. The shift from words and sense perceptions to simplicity and silence leads to union and communion with God.

The path towards union and communion with God begins with cataphatic theology but must end with apophatic theology. Professor Vladimir Lossky cites an ancient work, *Concerning Mystical Theology,* purportedly authored by Dionysius, a disciple of Saint Paul's, to introduce the distinction between these two theologies.

---

[265] Hierotheos, *The Illness and Cure of the Soul in the Orthodox Theology*, 95.

[266] Lossky, *Orthodox Theology: An Introduction*, 13.

[267] Vladimir Lossky, *In the Image and Likeness of God* (Crestwood, New York: St. Vladimir's Seminary Press, 1985), 91.

[268] Matthew 5:8 NASB.

[269] Lossky, *The Mystical Theology of the Eastern Church*, 8.

"One–that of cataphatic or positive theology–proceeds by affirmations; the other–apophatic or negative theology–by negations. The first leads us to some knowledge of God, but it is an imperfect way. The perfect way, the only way which is fitting in regard to God, who is of His very nature unknowable, is the second–which leads us finally to total ignorance."[270]

The two types of knowledge are positive and negative theology. Positive theology seeks to describe God in words and thoughts understandable to the human intellect. With positive knowledge, we claim to know certain things about God. Negative theology, on the other hand, realizes that any affirmative statement of God falls far short of His indescribable essence. Rather than talking about God, negative theology strives to experience not the essence but the energies of God. "The contrast between the two ways in the knowledge of God, between negative and positive theology, is for Dionysius founded upon this ineffable but real distinction between the unknowable essence and the self-revealing energies of the Divinity, between the 'unions' and the 'distinctions.'"[271] Whereas the "unions" present "the superessential nature of God where He remains as if in absolute repose, without manifesting Himself in any way," the "distinctions" are God's "processions" and "manifestations" given to us "in which everything that exists participates, thus making God known to His creatures."[272]

---

[270] Ibid., 25.
[271] Ibid., 72.
[272] Ibid.

Whereas the divine essence remains beyond our reach, we can receive the divine energies. "The goal of Orthodox spirituality, the blessedness of the Kingdom of Heaven, is not the vision of the essence, but, above all, a participation in the divine life of the Holy Trinity; the deified state of the co-heirs of the divine nature, gods created after the uncreated God, possessing by grace all that the Holy Trinity possesses by nature."[273] We can never perceive the essence of God; He remains infinite and uncreated. We may however through negative theology attempt to receive the grace of God Himself, through the experience of His freely gifted energies.

Positive theology by itself leads to pride. We think we can discover and contain God. "Without this use of the way of negation, of what is termed the apophatic approach, our talk about God becomes gravely misleading."[274] Positive theology divorced from apophatic theology presents innumerable attributes of God. These attributes by their very nature, however, inescapably attempt to put God in a box we control, so we can begin to get a handle on Him. This effort is futile, because God is infinite, while we are finite; God is uncreated, while we are created. God transcends human thought completely. With positive theology alone, we become proud of a knowledge falling infinitely short of the glory of God. We fool ourselves by trying to create God in our image, an exercise in futility doomed to utter failure.

---

[273] Lossky, *The Mystical Theology of the Eastern Church*, 65.
[274] Ware, *The Orthodox Way*, 14.

Negative theology, on the other hand, offers humanity a ray of hope. Rather than proudly boast about what we know about God, we walk in humility and honestly admit how little we know, how apart from God we can accomplish absolutely nothing of eternal significance. Whereas positive theology by itself provides spurious answers and false hope, negative theology leads to more questions about an unreachable God distinct from us in His being uncreated in infinity.

The seeker of God must embrace both positive and negative theology. Positive theology is a good start, but we must not end there. "Both theological paths are necessary for the knowledge of God. But the negative way is more perfect."[275] Apophatic theology opens our hearts and helps us to see. "The goal for the Christian is union with God in love."[276] To experience union and communion with God, we must "follow the correct Orthodox means and methodology, so as to be cured and encounter" life in Christ.[277] "The holy Fathers have presented this Orthodox method in their writings. It can be summarized in the three fundamental stages of the spiritual life: purification of heart, illumination of the nous and deification."[278]

---

[275] Lossky, *The Vision of God*, 125.

[276] Ibid., 116.

[277] Metropolitan Hierotheos of Nafpaktos, *The Illness and Cure of the Soul in the Orthodox Theology*, 2nd ed. rev., translated by Effie Mavromichali (Levadia, Greece: Birth of the Theotokos Monastery, 2010), 24-25.

[278] Ibid., 25.

"The purification of the heart is called praxis; the illumination of the nous is called natural theoria or simply theoria, because, through his illuminated nous, man sees the inner principles (logoi) of things in nature."[279] Purification requires repentance, where we put away the old man and become the new man of faith. According to Saint Maximos, the one passing through the stage of purification is freed from "sensual pleasure and pain."[280] These attributes are put to death: "What needs to be crucified is the things perceptible to the senses, and what needs to be buried is the world of our thoughts."[281]

Humanity "consists of the nous and the senses. Between the nous and sense perception lie imagination, opinion and mind. The nous is the centre of the soul, the eye of the soul."[282] Man can choose to sin, to repent, and to pray. When we sin, the nous is darkened because "each sin is a denial of Christ and indicates that a person's nous has been darkened."[283] When we repent, the darkness begins to dissipate. "When we pray, according to the advice of the holy Fathers, we attempt to keep our nous clear, 'imageless,' 'formless,' without fantasy. We do not imagine anything."[284] Pure prayer is the vehicle

---

[279] Ibid., 139.
[280] Ibid., 141.
[281] Ibid., 150-151.
[282] Ibid., 155.
[283] Ibid., 188.
[284] Ibid., 161.

towards God. "Only prayer combined with repentance purifies man and unites him with God."[285]

After purification, the uncreated grace of God can enter the human heart through the nous. "The nous (as) the eye of the soul… acquires experience of God."[286] The nous must be purified. "Anyone who purifies his nous, through repentance and the entire ascetic tradition of the Church, is illumined and noetic prayer starts at once. From this state a person can also attain to theoria of the uncreated Light, if God wills."[287] This process draws us closer to God. "Holy God imparts His uncreated energy to people and sanctifies them. He actually dwells in man by grace, and thus man becomes a dwelling place of the holy Triune God, a living temple of God."[288] Our goal remains a deep and abiding relationship with God. "A person is purified through noetic hesychia, and thus he is prepared for communion and union with God."[289]

"Knowledge of God is communion, union with God; it is theoria (vision) of God."[290] Yet repentance and the vision of God remain inextricably intertwined, for "the more one is united to Him, the more one becomes aware of His unknowability, and, in the same way, the more perfect one becomes, the more one is aware of one's own imperfection."[291]

---

[285] Ibid.

[286] Ibid., 81.

[287] Ibid., 186.

[288] Ibid., 60-61.

[289] Ibid., 147.

[290] Ibid., 127.

[291] Lossky, *The Mystical Theology of the Eastern Church*, 205.

"For those who are near God, the greatest knowledge is the knowledge of their own ignorance."[292] We believe we know so much by what we think with our minds and perceive with our senses. Yet this intellectual activity does not bring us to God; rather it brings us an image of God, an image falling infinitely short because our feeble mind and flawed senses spring from our finite and created nature, while God remains infinite and uncreated. "Knowledge of God can only be attained by going beyond every visible and intelligible object. It is by ignorance that we know the One who is above all that can be an object of knowledge. It is no divine gnosis which is the supreme end, but the union that surpasses all knowledge."[293] "In the state of union we know God at a higher level than intelligence–νοῦς–for the simple reason that we do not know Him at all."[294]

"The goal to which apophatic theology leads–if, indeed, we may speak of goal or ending when, as here, it is a question of an ascent towards the infinite; this infinite goal is not a nature or an essence, nor is it a person; it is something which transcends all notion both of nature and of person: it is the Trinity."[295] "The Trinity is, for the Orthodox Church, the unshakeable foundation of all religious thought, of all piety, of all spiritual life, of all experience. It is the Trinity that we seek in seeking after God,

---

[292] Lossky, *The Vision of God*, 92.
[293] Ibid., 122.
[294] Ibid., 123.
[295] Lossky, *The Mystical Theology of the Eastern Church*, 44.

when we search for the fullness of being, for the end and meaning of existence."[296]

Genuine contemplation leads to a vision of God. In this regard, man begins to pray with words and thoughts but strives to find God in the silence. "When a person is purified, he is delivered from the images of fantasies."[297] Gone are the images, gone is the imagination, and prayer becomes without passion and preconception. "Here wordless, contemplative prayer begins; the prayer in which the heart lays itself open in silence before God."[298] Although we cannot know God in His essence, we can perceive Him in His energies. "To see God is to contemplate the Trinity while fully participating in His light."[299] Prayer to God and love for God become one. "The fruit of prayer is divine love, which is simply grace, appropriated in the depth of our being."[300]

"Therefore, since we have so great a cloud of witnesses surrounding us, let us also lay aside every encumbrance and the sin which so easily entangles us, and let us run with endurance the race that is set before us, fixing our eyes on Jesus, the author and perfecter of faith, who for the joy set before Him endured the cross, despising the shame, and has sat down at the right hand of the throne of

---

[296] Ibid., 65.

[297] Hierotheos, *The Illness and Cure of the Soul in the Orthodox Theology*, 93.

[298] Lossky, *The Mystical Theology of the Eastern Church*, 206.

[299] Lossky, *The Vision of God*, 81.

[300] Lossky, *The Mystical Theology of the Eastern Church*, 206.

God."[301] This cloud of witnesses becomes our role models describing how we should live our faith every minute of every day. We want to be like our heroes the saints because they were so close to God here on earth and now are infinitely closer to God in heaven.

Each Saturday, we prepare our hearts for the Divine Liturgy by reminding ourselves how prayer is exemplified in the lives of the saints. Like the saints we love, we practice the Virtue of Prayer throughout the day, culminating in our communal celebration of Saturday evening Vespers and, at Saint Patrick Orthodox Church, Benediction and Adoration. Prayer becomes second nature, reflecting who we are rather than something we do.

---

[301] Hebrews 12:1-2 NASB.

CHAPTER SEVEN

SUNDAY

THE VIRTUE OF JOY

"He who eats My flesh and drinks
My blood abides in Me, and I in him"
(John 6:56 NASB).

Sunday, recalling the Resurrection, is the most joyful day for Orthodox Christians. Our desire for God never can be fulfilled completely, but on Sunday we receive the Body and Blood of Christ in Holy Communion. Definitely the highlight of my week each week, the Eucharist embodies the Virtue of Joy.

As a Wesleyan pastor in southern Indiana prior to coming home to Orthodoxy, I celebrated our simple Christmas Eve service at our little church in 2009 and was blessed beyond measure. On other occasions, I spent hours with Bobby, a World War Two veteran and former P.O.W. captured by Nazi Germany, sharing the Good News of Jesus Christ during visits at his home. I hoped these talks would build a personal relationship with him, with the goal of eventually bringing him back into our church. Only a few attended our Christmas Eve service that night, but amazingly, Bobby was one of them, and that brought great joy to my heart. This was the only time I ever saw him in church, and a few months later I preached his funeral.

That Christmas Eve was special for another reason. I yearned for many days and even during our evening service to go to Midnight Mass that night. I decided to continue this long-treasured tradition, begun in my Roman Catholic childhood, with a late-night journey to Saint Michael Orthodox Church in Louisville during that Christmas Eve once the last of my congregation left our church earlier that evening.

Orthodoxy has been described by many as the best kept secret in America. I discovered Orthodoxy very late in life. A year shy of my 50th birthday, several months after my ordination, I interviewed for a teaching position at a school associated with Saint Mark Coptic Orthodox Church in Fairfax, Virginia. The Christian school where I taught and coached for five years was closing, and I sought another teaching assignment at a new school. During the interview, Coptic priest Father Anthony Messeh drew a simple picture that changed my life. Beginning with the first century, Father Anthony drew with a straight line how the Orthodox Church moved upward towards the twenty-first century, and in the split known as the Great Schism, the West departed from the straight and constant line of the East, veering to the right. Further deviations upon this wayward line occurred during the Protestant Reformation, yet the Eastern Orthodox Church traveled straight and strong. As a former Roman Catholic and current Protestant pastor, I was stunned by this depiction of Church history and said, "Father, if what you say is true, my entire worldview is destroyed." Father Anthony gave five Orthodox books to me. I taught for a couple years at a different school before becoming the lead pastor at a Wesleyan church in southern Indiana. During most of these intervening years, the five books sat unopened on my bookshelf, but one by one they eventually were read, and on that Christmas Eve in 2009, my heart yearned to return to Midnight Mass.

The Nativity Eve Divine Liturgy at Saint Michael Orthodox Church in Louisville brought me back to the gold and glitter, the magnificence and mystery of my childhood faith. The very next day, I drove back to Louisville to attend Matins at the Saint George Chapel at the same site and found myself surprised we were all standing with no chairs, and I was lost completely during the service. Father Alexander Atty of blessed memory came to my assistance and generously offered his copy of the Daily Service book for me to keep.

Father Alexander showed kindness to me that morning and in several other encounters during the next few years as he battled the scourge of cancer with courage and grace. I once asked him specifically what he wanted me to pray for during his sickness, and he thought for a few seconds before responding, "Peace. Praying for healing gets old after a while."[302] On another occasion Father

---

[302] Alexander Atty, "The Prodigal Son," Vespers, Saint Raphael of Brooklyn Orthodox Church, Chantilly, VA, 24 March 2012. Lecture.

Thomas Palke of Saint Raphael of Brooklyn Orthodox Church invited me to hear Father Alexander address his congregation, and he spoke eloquently about the Prodigal Son. Father Alexander talked about how earlier he was going to face a ten-hour cancer surgery with the thought that he "may not make it." He engaged in a life confession lasting three to four hours and concluded his talk to us by saying, "Illness was a great gift to me. God gave me a great gift: cancer. It taught me to prepare for death every day."[303]

My Indiana Wesleyan pastorate brought an additional encounter with Orthodoxy. I was honoured and humbled to meet Father Peter Gillquist of blessed memory. At the Cracker Barrel in Bloomington, Indiana, with Father Peter and his son Father Peter Jon, he spoke lovingly about the Blessed Virgin Mary, rekindling another deep love from my childhood long-dormant during my Protestant pastoral assignments. Father Peter saw the Theotokos in the Burning Bush and in other Scriptural passages in the Old Testament, another startling viewpoint I never considered before. I continued my pastoral ministry with the Wesleyans for the next few years in Virginia, but each summer I would return to All Saints Orthodox Church in Bloomington, Indiana, to worship with the wonderful people there and talk to Father Peter about the status of my Orthodox journey. His untimely death to cancer was another painful loss for so many of us, and each summer I still enjoy visiting Father Peter Jon and his mother

---

[303] Ibid.

Khouria Marilyn Gillquist and their superb congregation in my home state.

I met one other giant of the faith during my journey into Orthodoxy, listening to and meeting His Eminence Metropolitan Kallistos Ware at Saint Mark Coptic Orthodox Church during the summer of 2012. Metropolitan Kallistos spoke about how to incorporate the Jesus Prayer into our daily lives. As described so eloquently by Metropolitan Kallistos during his talk, like Moses at the Burning Bush, we Orthodox stand on holy ground, and our faith is immersed in awe and wonder. God created us to pray, and without prayer in our lives we are not fully human. During our prayerful silence, we listen intently for the presence of God. From the stillness of prayer, Jesus offered words of fire and healing, acts of power and transformation. Like Jesus, from the silence and stillness of our prayer, we embrace others with words of healing, with acts of love.

What I especially remember about his talk was Metropolitan Kallistos quoting one of my favorite authors, Antoine de Saint-Exupéry writing in *The Little Prince*, "And now here is my secret, a very simple secret: It is only with the heart that one can see rightly; what is essential is invisible to the eye."[304] As mentioned before, these words, more than any others, best express my lifelong journey into Orthodoxy. More than anything, this journey has been one from the head to the heart, from the innocence and wonder of my Roman Catholic upbringing to the

---

[304] Saint-Exupéry, *The Little Prince*, 73.

experience of God through the Divine Liturgy in the Orthodox Church.

As I transferred from my church in Indiana to join another Wesleyan congregation in Virginia, Father Peter Gillquist of blessed memory offered one additional gift to me. He suggested I contact Father Patrick Cardine and Father Thomas Palke in Virginia. For nearly a decade I had lived in downtown Warrenton, Virginia, and Saint Patrick Orthodox Church, a mission church at the time, was meeting in the back of an antique mall in Warrenton. Father Patrick spent countless hours listening to my journey and sharing the truth of Orthodoxy. The loving people of his church made me feel right at home, and Father Patrick, Khouria Kerrie, and their six wonder-filled children opened their hearts and home to offer an abundance of love and joy to this pilgrim. For nearly three years as a Wesleyan assistant pastor, I would be welcomed into Saint Patrick Orthodox Church on the nights I was free to join their worship services, filled with joy except for my sadness at not being able to receive Holy Communion. Exclusion from the Eucharist was necessary yet painful, leaving an exquisite emptiness deep in my heart. Most fittingly, I finally was anointed with the Holy Chrism on the Feast of the Nativity of the Blessed Virgin Mary on Sunday 8 September 2013. Father Patrick chose the name "Nicodemus" for me because, like my protégé in John 3, as a Protestant pastor I visited his church in secret and in the dead of night.

There has been an abundance of joy in the journey into Orthodoxy. Father Alexander Atty of blessed memory taught me to live life to the fullest, in Christ and with Mary, because each day is a gift from God, another opportunity to love. Father Peter Gillquist of blessed memory taught me to love and reverence Our Lady, rekindling in my heart a deep and abiding love and reverence for the Theotokos present in my earliest childhood memories when I best walked by a simple yet profound faith, the faith of a child in love with God. Metropolitan Kallistos Ware taught me to see with the inner eyes of faith, to continue my move from the head to the heart, to embrace Orthodoxy in all her mysterious joy and wonder. Fathers Patrick Cardine and Thomas Palke shared the Orthodox faith and welcomed me into their churches.

If you were born Orthodox, you need to thank your parents and family. If you like me are a convert, you need to thank those extraordinary men and women, those pillars of faith, leading you into the truth of Orthodoxy. Whether native or convert, we are all called in Christ with Mary to pray with joy and thanksgiving: "Rejoice always; pray without ceasing; in everything give thanks, for this is God's will for you in Christ Jesus."[305]

The absolute highlight of my week, each and every week of my life as an Orthodox Christian, occurs on Sunday when I receive the Eucharist. During the Canon of the Mass during our Western Rite Divine Liturgy at Saint Patrick Orthodox Church, we proclaim in faith as did Saint Thomas the Apostle, deep in our hearts upon seeing the consecrated Body and Blood of Christ, "My Lord and

---

[305] 1 Thessalonians 5:16-18 NASB.

my God."[306] Going to Holy Communion and receiving the Holy Eucharist during the Divine Liturgy is the very best way I know to meet the Incarnate God. "The Eucharist is this: the memory made sacrament, the presence experienced, the moment made eternal, the bread and wine, the flesh and blood. But first of all, the Eucharist is memory."[307]

"Through the sacrament of the Holy Eucharist, God enters into union with the whole man."[308] Baptism is only the beginning of our wonder-filled Orthodox journey of faith. After the baptismal cleansing, we are guided towards sanctity by the Holy Chrism and nurtured in our new life in Christ by the Holy Eucharist. "The Holy Eucharist preserves and continues" our new life in Christ.[309] In this regard, the Body and Blood of Christ preserves our baptismal innocence and draws us closer to God. "God has chosen us not for death, but for life, whose *telos* or ultimate goal is eternal communion with the Persons of the Holy Trinity."[310]

The Joy of Orthodoxy occurs when we move beyond a mere knowledge of God into a mystical experience of the Trinity during each Divine Liturgy. "If you have a living priest, a living choir and a living congregation, then you

---

[306] John 20:28 NASB.

[307] Metropolitan Philip Saliba and Joseph Allen, *Meeting the Incarnate God*, 39.

[308] Allen, *And He Leads Them*, 93.

[309] Cabasilas, *The Life in Christ*, 50.

[310] John Breck, *The Sacred Gift of Life* (Crestwood, New York: St. Vladimir's Seminary Press, 1998), 215.

will find yourself involved in a wonderful mystical experience."[311] Our two-hour celebration of Matins and Mass each Sunday morning at St. Patrick Orthodox Church deepens my walk with God and empowers me to face the vocational challenges in my life with joy and grace. "The grace of the Lord Jesus Christ, and the love of God, and the communion of the Holy Spirit *be* with you all. Amen."[312] With these words, Saint Paul the Apostle concludes his final letter to the church in Corinth. Trinitarian doctrine permeates the Johannine and Pauline theologies within the Orthodox Church.

"The chief source of our knowledge of the Trinity is, indeed, none other than the Prologue of Saint John (and also the first epistle of the same), and that is why the author of these amazing texts has received, in the Orthodox tradition, the name of St. John the Theologian."[313] Saint John the Theologian begins his Gospel with these memorable words, "In the beginning was the Word, and the Word was with God, and the Word was God."[314] The miracle of the Incarnation, the Word of God Who is God becoming flesh, best expresses Saint John's Trinitarian theology. In this regard, "He Who is incarnated is indeed none other than the Word, that is to say, the second person of the Trinity. Incarnation and Trinity are thus inseparable."[315]

---

[311] Allen, *And He Leads Them*, 95.
[312] 2 Corinthians 13:14 NKJV.
[313] Lossky, *Orthodox Theology: An Introduction*, 36.
[314] John 1:1 NKJV.
[315] Lossky, *Orthodox Theology: An Introduction*, 36.

Saint John the Theologian declares that "the Word was with God, and the Word was God."[316] Because the Word was with God, the Father and the Son are distinct but related. Because the Word was God, the second person of the Trinity possesses the fullness of divinity. Because "the Word became flesh,"[317] the second person of the Trinity, besides being fully God, also is fully man.

Besides introducing the second person of the Trinity, Saint John the Theologian also introduces the Holy Spirit, the third person of the Trinity. Jesus tells His disciples after the Last Supper, "And I will pray the Father, and he shall give you another Comforter, that he may abide with you for ever; *Even* the Spirit of truth."[318] Jesus explains to His closest followers the mission of the Holy Spirit when He says, "But the Comforter, which is the Holy Ghost, whom the Father will send in my name, he shall teach you all things, and bring all things to your remembrance, whatsoever I have said unto you."[319] "The Son and the Spirit thus appear, throughout the Gospel, as two divine persons sent into the world, the former to quicken our personal liberty, the latter to unite Itself to our nature and regenerate it."[320] Both God the Son and God the Holy Spirit are "equal in dignity to the Father and identical to Him in substance."[321]

---

[316] John 1:1 NKJV.
[317] John 1:14 NASB.
[318] John 14:16-17a KJV.
[319] John 14:26 KJV.
[320] Lossky, *Orthodox Theology: An Inroduction*, 39.
[321] Ibid.

Saint Paul the Apostle develops Trinitarian doctrine even further through his epistles or letters written to the various New Testament churches. One of his most sublime passages describes the second person of the Trinity: "He is the image of the invisible God, the firstborn over all creation."[322] With these words, "Paul states the perfect resemblance of the Son to the Father, through a unique filiation."[323] The Greek word for "image" is *eikon*, from which we in the Orthodox tradition develop the theology of iconography. Just as Jesus Christ mirrors His heavenly Father, the Church calls us to conform our lives in obedience to the life of Jesus Christ the Son of the Father. Just as the Christ "is the image of the invisible God, the firstborn of all creation,"[324] so too are we "predestined to be conformed to the image of His Son, that He might be the firstborn of many brethren."[325] Although "we do not know what we should pray for as we ought, but the Spirit Himself makes intercession for us with groaning which cannot be uttered."[326]

Trinitarian theology permeates the writings of Saint Paul in the New Testament. "The headwords of the Pauline epistles show a solemn usage of the divine name as Father, in a benediction of a truly liturgical character."[327] Paul's epistles begin with a salutation in the name of God

---

[322] Colossians 1:15 NKJV.
[323] Bobrinskoy, *The Mystery of the Trinity*, 123.
[324] Colossians 1:15 NKJV.
[325] Romans 8:29 NASB.
[326] Romans 8:26 NKJV.
[327] Bobrinskoy, *The Mystery of the Trinity*, 108.

the Father and Jesus Christ His Son, and "the work of the Spirit consists of professing the Name and the Lordship of Jesus Christ in the Christian community."[328] Our Orthodox journey begins in the baptismal waters. "The entire new life in the Spirit, all the love of the Father poured into our hearts, culminates in the baptismal experience of the grace of Christ."[329] Saint Paul preaches Christ crucified and risen from the dead; indeed, God the Father "did not spare His own Son"[330] and "raised up Jesus our Lord from the dead."[331] Salvation lies at the heart of the Pauline epistles, for "if you confess with your mouth Jesus *as* Lord, and believe in your heart that God raised Him from the dead, you shall be saved."[332] Such a heartfelt declaration, that Jesus Christ is Lord, requires the active presence of the Holy Spirit in one's life, because "no man can say that Jesus in the Lord, but by the Holy Ghost."[333]

Within the Pauline tradition, the Epistle to the Hebrews describes how the second person of the Trinity interrelates with God the Father. In this regard, the Son of God is perceived as "the radiance of His glory and the exact representation of His nature, and upholds all things by the word of His power. When He had made purification of sins, He sat down at the right hand of the Majesty

---

[328] Ibid., 114.
[329] Ibid.
[330] Romans 8:32a NKJV.
[331] Romans 4:24 KJV.
[332] Romans 10:9a NKJV.
[333] 1 Corinthians 12:3b KJV.

on high."[334] Sitting at the right hand of God expresses "a relationship of equality" between God the Father and God the Son, portraying "the Son's magnificent honor."[335] For this reason and returning to Johannine theology, Jesus boldly declares, "Believe me that I *am* in the Father, and the Father in me,"[336] and even more forcefully proclaims, "I and *my* Father are one."[337]

Our union and communion with the Triune God reach fruition in the reception of the Eucharist during the Divine Liturgy: "He that eateth my flesh, and drinketh my blood, dwelleth in me, and I in him. As the living Father hath sent me, and I live by the Father; so he that eateth me, even he shall live by me."[338] During the Last Supper Discourse later in the Gospel of Saint John, Jesus vividly describes for His disciples this union and communion with God: "That they all may be one; as thou, Father, *art* in me, and I in thee, that they also may be one in us: that the world may believe that thou hast sent me."[339] Our faith will grow through the power and presence of the Holy Spirit in our lives: "But the Comforter, *which is* the Holy Ghost, whom the Father will send in my name, he shall teach you all things, and bring all things to your remembrance, whatsoever I have said unto you."[340]

---

[334] Hebrews 1:3 NKJV.

[335] Saint Basil, *On the Holy Spirit*, 41.

[336] John 14:11a KJV.

[337] John 10:30 KJV.

[338] John 6:56-57 KJV.

[339] John 17:21 KJV.

[340] John 14:26 KJV.

Our union and communion with the Holy Trinity become our deepest and truest sources of joy in our lives. For Saint John the Theologian, whereas Jesus is the "only begotten Son" of the Father,[341] the Holy Spirit "proceeds from the Father."[342] The Holy Spirit inspires us. "The essential fruit of the Spirit, the fullness of His presence, is unceasing praise and thanksgiving to God in Jesus Christ."[343] Saint John and Saint Paul lay the groundwork for the later Trinitarian professions of faith in the fourth century and our recognition that the essence of the Trinity is a mystery infinitely beyond our feeble human comprehension. Yet God calls us to seek and contemplate the unknowable: "The way, then, to knowledge of God, is from the one Spirit, through the one Son, to the one Father."[344]

A trend in second-century ecclesiology is the emerging consciousness of the presence of God in the life of the Church. According to Saint Justin Martyr, the term "holy" describes the Church aptly because it "expresses the conviction that it is God's chosen people and is indwelt by His Spirit."[345] According to Saint Ignatius, because "the incarnation is the union of seen with unseen, flesh with spirit, ... the Church is at once flesh and Spirit, its unity being the union of both."[346] In this regard, "it is

[341] John 3:16.
[342] John 15:26.
[343] Bobrinskoy, *The Mystery of the Trinity*, 107.
[344] Saint Basil, *On the Holy Spirit*, 83.
[345] Kelly, *Early Christian Doctrines*, 190.
[346] Ibid., 190-191.

a holy community within which the divine Spirit lives and operates."[347]

This results in the greatest joy of all. "And above everything else we shall–with fear and joy, spiritual trembling and faith–rediscover the Sacrament of Christ's Body and Blood as the very source and the constant focus of our life as Christians!"[348]

The heart of John's Gospel describes this incarnational mystery: "And the Word became flesh, and dwelt among us, and we saw His glory, glory as of the only begotten from the Father, full of grace and truth."[349] The Word is Jesus, and the Word is God.[350] The word "flesh" in John 1:14 is the Greek word *sarx*. John could have written, "the Word became a man," using the Greek work *anthropos*, but he goes deeper, using this harsher word *sarx* to reinforce the incarnational mystery of God becoming man. In the sixth chapter of John, this powerful word appears six times, half the total uses in the entire Gospel.[351] The language of this harsh word *sarx* jars us further when Jesus challenges His listeners and us to "eat the flesh of the Son of man, and drink his blood."[352] The stark and potent image continues with flesh and blood mentioned twice

....

[347] Ibid., 191.

[348] Alexander Schmemann, *Great Lent* (Crestwood, NY: St. Vladimir's Seminary Press, 1969), 133.

[349] John 1:14 NASB.

[350] John 1:1 NASB.

[351] Jerome Kodell, *The Eucharist in the New Testament* (Collegeville, MN: Liturgical Press, 1991), 125.

[352] John 6:53 KJV.

more in the next two verses.[353] In addition, the Greek word for eat in the next two verses has the vulgar connotation of gnaw.[354] The Real Presence of Christ in the Eucharistic bread and wine is affirmed in a dramatic way. In addition, the Eucharist offers each participant in the Divine Liturgy the chance to experience personal union and communion with Christ in His divine mission of salvation.[355] This promise of Jesus is brilliant beyond belief: "He that eateth my flesh, and drinketh my blood, dwelleth in me, and I in him."[356] Best of all for us attending the Divine Liturgy each Sunday, "This indwelling is sacramentalized and strengthened in the Eucharist."[357]

Another source of great joy in our lives is the Holy Sacraments, especially our regular reception of Holy Communion. Baptism and the Eucharist are interconnected. The Holy Spirit cleaves to a person at the moment of baptism.[358] Baptism confers being and initiates our existence in Christ.[359] The anointing with Holy Chrism perfects the new believer in Christ[360] as he or she is filled with the indwelling Holy Spirit. After the baptismal cleansing, we are guided towards sanctity by the Holy Chrism and nurture our new life in Christ by the Holy Eucharist. "The

---

[353] John 6:54-55 KJV.
[354] Kodell, *The Eucharist in the New Testament*, 125.
[355] Ibid.
[356] John 6:56 KJV.
[357] Kodell, *The Eucharist in the New Testament*, 126.
[358] Mantzaridis, *The Deification of Man*, 64.
[359] Cabasilas, *The Life in Christ*, 49.
[360] Ibid., 50.

Holy Eucharist preserves and continues" our new life in Christ,[361] the Body and Blood of Christ preserving our baptismal innocence and continuing our new life in fullness and grace.

Baptism and the Eucharist stand as the premier sacraments of the Church. Whereas we "put on Christ"[362] in Baptism, we receive the Body and Blood of Christ in the Eucharist. Through both sacraments, we find ourselves "dead to sin but alive to God in Christ Jesus."[363] Through the sacrament of Baptism, we are born anew of water and the Spirit, entering God's kingdom.[364] Similarly, Saint Ignatius of Antioch describes the Eucharist as a medicine for our immorality or new life in Christ.[365]

The rite of Baptism parallels the Eucharistic prayer of thanksgiving. Both Baptism and the Eucharist begin with a solemn doxology to the Father, Son, and Holy Spirit.[366] These sacraments may be divided into four parts: Preface, Anamnesis, Epiclesis, and Consecration. The baptismal Preface hearkens back to the beginning, to creation, with words of thanksgiving, similar to the Preface in the Eucharistic prayer.[367] The baptismal Anamnesis remembers the saving acts of God manifested in His Kingdom.[368] This

---

[361] Cabasilas, *The Life in Christ*, 50.
[362] Galatians 3:27 NKJV.
[363] Romans 6:11 NIV.
[364] Walker *et al*, *A History of the Christian Church*, 105.
[365] Ibid., 109.
[366] Schmemann, *Of Water & the Spirit*, 40.
[367] Ibid., 46.
[368] Ibid., 47.

resembles the Eucharist as humanity experiences communion with Christ. The Epiclesis in both Baptism and the Eucharist invokes the Holy Spirit. The priest asks God to sanctify the baptismal water with the indwelling Holy Spirit, and he asks the Holy Spirit to come down upon the gifts of bread and wine and the people of God during the Canon of the Mass. Finally, the Consecration of both Baptism and the Eucharist use a similar formula. Whereas in Baptism the priest invokes God, " 'O Master of all, *show this water* to be the water of redemption, the water of sanctification, the purification of flesh and spirit,"[369] the priest asks God within the Eucharistic prayer of Saint Basil to "show this bread as the very precious Body.'"[370]

Both Baptism and the Eucharist point ahead to the *parousia*. God does not replace the created elements of water in Baptism and bread and wine in the Eucharist with supernatural or sacred material. On the contrary, matter is restored to a place of communion with God. In this regard, the holy water of Baptism and the bread and wine in the Eucharist represent the whole of creation as it will become in the eschaton, at the end, "when it will be consummated in God, when He will fill all things in Himself."[371]

Both Baptism and the Eucharist invite us to "pass over" into the Kingdom of God. As the water of Baptism is holy through the presence of Christ and the Holy Spirit, the

---

[369] Ibid., 49 (emphasis in original).
[370] Ibid.
[371] Ibid.

bread and wine in the Eucharist are truly "the Body and Blood of Christ, His *parousia*, His presence among us."[372] As a result, the gates are opened for our union with God. The sacraments of Baptism and Eucharist are means to the end, the end being our deification in Christ, our knowledge of and communion with God.[373]

The Divine Liturgy is the ultimate highlight of my week, and the reception of the Body and Blood of Christ is for me the highlight of the Mass. The Eucharist stands as the "source and goal of the entire liturgical life of the Church."[374] Throughout the Synoptic Gospel and Pauline Epistle Last Supper accounts, and especially in light of the Bread of Life Discourse in the Gospel of John, Jesus shared Himself with His disciples in an intimate way.[375] In effect, by offering His Body and Blood, Jesus offered Himself.

Saint Irenaeus' ecclesiology includes his description of the Eucharist as "the new oblation of the new covenant."[376] This sacrifice is received from the apostles and offered to God throughout the entire world.[377] Our discussion comes full circle. Whereas Tertullian reflects upon the divine and human substances of Jesus Christ, both God and man,

---

[372] Ibid., 50.
[373] Ibid.
[374] Schmemann, *Introduction to Liturgical Theology*, 24.
[375] Kodell, *The Eucharist in the New Testament*, 21.
[376] Kelly, *Early Christian Doctrines*, 196.
[377] Ibid.

"Irenaeus teaches that the bread and wine are really the Lord's body and blood."[378]

Every Sunday, we need to recall the Eucharistic celebration and realize we experience the presence of Christ in a unique way each time we receive Holy Communion. This intimate union and communion in Christ can be recalled and remembered every minute of every day and truly epitomize the Virtue of Joy.

---

[378] Ibid., 198.

EPILOGUE

LIVING THE VIRTUOUS LIFE EACH DAY

But the LORD said to Samuel, "Do not look on his appearance or on the height of his stature, because I have rejected him; for the LORD does not see as mortals see; they look on the outward appearance, but the LORD looks on the heart" (1 Samuel 16:7 NRSV).

Peter, James, and John, the disciples on Mount Tabor, were dazzled by the brilliant glory of God and could see and understand only to the extent of their limited yet growing faith. The Orthodox Church Service Book for "The Transfiguration of Our Lord and God and Saviour Jesus Christ" on 6 August presents this epic event brilliantly: "Thou wast transfigured upon the mountain, O Christ our God, showing Thy glory to Thy disciples as far as they were able to bear it."[379]

---

[379] *The Festal Menaion*, translated by Mother Mary and Kallistos Ware (South Canaan, PA: St. Tikhon's Seminary Press, 1969), 477-478.

The glorified body of Jesus on Mount Tabor anticipates our own transfigured life in Christ. "Today Christ on Mount Tabor has changed the darkened nature of Adam, and filling it with brightness He has made it godlike."[380] The process of *theosis* or deification involves God becoming man so that man could become like God. The gap between God and man seems insurmountable at first glance: "The closer one is to God the more conscious he becomes of the ontological unworthiness of all creatures before God, of the totally free gift of God."[381] The Paschal Mystery, the movement from sin and death to resurrection and life, is made possible because humanity is made holy in the Transfiguration: "For in His mercy the Saviour of our souls has transfigured disfigured man and made him shine with light upon Mount Tabor."[382]

A small glimpse of what humanity could become is revealed in the Transfiguration. "Our new life in Christ is not another life, or a different life, but the same life renewed, transformed, and transfigured by the Holy Spirit."[383] When we approach life using our own power, our lives are small, and our impact is limited. Great things begin to happen with an eternal impact, however, when Christ begins to live and work through us: "I have been crucified with Christ; and it is no longer I who live, but Christ lives in me."[384] A virtuous life pursued in Christ

---

[380] Ibid., 469.
[381] Schmemann, *Great Lent*, 119-120.
[382] *The Festal Menaion*, 468.
[383] Schmemann, *Of Water & the Spirit*, 107.
[384] Galatians 2:20 NASB.

leads to future glory: "When Thou wast transfigured, O Saviour, upon a high mountain, having with Thee the chief disciples, Thou hast shone forth in glorious majesty, proving thereby that those who surpass in the height of their virtues shall be worthy of the divine glory."[385]

Whereas Moses saw the back of God on Mount Sinai in the Old Testament, the disciples saw the glory of God on Mount Tabor in the New Testament. "For thy dread Transfiguration, the mystery hidden before the ages, has been made manifest in the last times to Peter, John, and James."[386] Both of these historical events portend the eschatological coming of Christ when we shall see His future glory. According to Saint Gregory Palamas, the light of the transfiguration both manifests Christ's divine nature and symbolizes the glory of the age to come.[387] "Thou wast transfigured upon Mount Tabor, showing the exchange mortal men will make with Thy glory at Thy second and fearful coming."[388]

The Transfiguration revealed the divine hidden within the humanity of Jesus. "He, indeed, assumed humanity that we might become God."[389] With these words, the great Saint Athanasius describes the doctrine of deification or *theosis*.

In order to change humanity from the inside-out, to offer a cure for our troubled souls, "theology must be praise

---

[385] *The Festal Menaion*, 470.

[386] Ibid., 471.

[387] Mantzaridis, *The Deification of Man*, 97.

[388] *The Festal Menaion*, 478.

[389] Saint Athanasius, *On the Incarnation*, 93.

and must dispose us to praise God."[390] God reveals Himself both in Sacred Scripture and in the person of Jesus Christ, fully God and fully man. The Incarnation linked divinity and humanity like never before. "The source of true Christian theology is thus the confession of the Incarnation of the Son of God. Through the Incarnation, indeed, a person unites in himself the transcendent, unknowable nature of divinity, to human nature."[391] We respond to God's revelation in faith and with love, an active faith beyond mere belief and a deepening love of God and neighbor. Going beyond how we act or what we know, Orthodox theology addresses who we are in relationship with God. We experience God and seek to be more like Christ. Our primary purpose is not to learn more about God but rather to become more like God. As just stated, "He, indeed, assumed humanity that we might become God."[392]

Orthodox theology is not a philosophical system but a way of life. "The holy Fathers have presented this Orthodox method in their writings. It can be summarized in the three fundamental stages of the spiritual life: purification of heart, illumination of the nous and deification."[393] If Orthodoxy stays pure and remains true to her rich liturgical and ascetical tradition, she can avoid becoming a

---

[390] Lossky, *Orthodox Theology: An Introduction*, 14.

[391] Ibid., 34.

[392] Saint Athanasius, *On the Incarnation*, 93.

[393] Hierotheos, *The Illness and Cure of the Soul in the Orthodox Theology,* 25 (footnote omitted).

simple philosophical system by offering her people a real cure for their souls.

For the Orthodox theologian as spiritual therapist, "illness is the darkening of the nous."[394] For the Orthodox Christian, "the nous is the core of man's spiritual world, the eye of the soul."[395] If the nous is darkened, the soul is impure. If the nous is pure, the soul may become pure. "Blessed are the pure in heart: for they shall see God."[396] Orthodox theology moves beyond philosophy by promoting a deeper communion with God. In this regard, "in Orthodox theology, healing is associated with union with God, with the vision of God, the attainment of deification, which is identified with theoria of God."[397]

Evagrius Ponticus, a fourth-century monk, described how the nous guides us towards the truth of the Trinity. "In the act of contemplating God, the human intelligence comprehends itself, it sees itself in seeing Him. This perception is simultaneous: in knowing God, the νοῦς knows itself as the place of God's presence, as a receptacle for the light of the Trinity."[398] According to Saint Gregory of Nyssa, this seeking after God culminates in indescribable love. "Desiring God more and more, the soul grows without ceasing, going beyond herself and outside herself; and in the measure in which she unites herself more and more to

---

[394] Ibid., 62.

[395] Ibid., 156.

[396] Matthew 5:8 KJV.

[397] Hierotheos, *The Illness and Cure of the Soul in the Orthodox Theology*, 62.

[398] Lossky, *In the Image and Likeness of God*, 35.

God, her love becomes more ardent and insatiable."[399] Orthodox theology avoids the traps of philosophical systems to the extent it focuses our hearts on a deep and abiding union and communion with God.

Orthodox gnosiology must transcend philosophy and intellectual inquiry and touch our hearts in the phenomenological, existential, ontological, personal, and mystical realms. Phenomenologically, our subjective experience of God is more relevant than what we know about God. Existentially, we begin as a finite and created being in search of an infinite and uncreated God. Ontologically, we are human and called to become Christ-like, transformed from the inside-out by uncreated grace. As a person, we are unique, created in the image and likeness of God, and our ultimate goal in life is union and communion with one God, the three persons of the Trinity. Mystically, God touches and moves our soul beyond anything we can imagine or accomplish through our finite human efforts.

God exists as infinite and uncreated, and we always will be finite and created. While we cannot know the essence of God, we can know His energies. God is a personal God who loved the world so much, He sent His "only begotten Son" Jesus to live in our presence and give us "everlasting life."[400] By faith I not only believe but seek to become more Christ-like. "This mystery of faith as personal encounter and ontological participation is the unique foundation of

---

[399] Ibid., 37.
[400] John 3:16 KJV.

theological language."[401] From there, faith takes us into the mystical realm.

Although we still remain creatures, we are called to become "partakers of the divine nature."[402] As creatures, we can never attain full union and communion with the divine essence. Whereas we are creatures, God is, has been, and will always be uncreated. Yet we still may partake in the divine nature through our union with the divine energies. Within Orthodox theology, the uncreated Christ possesses both a hypostatic union with His divine nature and a substantial union within the Trinity.[403] As created beings, we obtain neither hypostatic nor substantial union with God; our union occurs within the realm of the divine energies. This union by grace makes us participants in the divine nature, through the divine energies, without losing our essence in the divine essence of God.[404] Just as Christ remained God while becoming man through the mystery of the Incarnation, we "remain creatures while becoming God by grace."[405] Again we return to our love for the Holy Trinity. "The goal of Orthodox spirituality, the blessedness of the Kingdom of Heaven, is not the vision of the essence, but, above all, a participation in the divine life of the Holy Trinity."[406]

---

[401] Lossky, *Orthodox Theology: An Introduction*, 25.

[402] 2 Peter 1:4 NASB.

[403] Lossky, *The Mystical Theology of the Eastern Church*, 87.

[404] Ibid.

[405] Ibid.

[406] Ibid., 65.

Bringing our discussion down to earth, how do you begin to participate in this divine life of the Trinity? Perhaps you start at the heart of Orthodox theology, through a full and active participation in the Divine Liturgy. As a deacon, I realize books, ascetic practice, and prayer are all essential, but the ongoing reception of the Holy Eucharist within the communal celebration of our Holy Mass at Saint Patrick Orthodox Church is a better, maybe even the best, way for me to experience God. "He that eateth my flesh, and drinketh my blood, dwelleth in me, and I in him."[407] As a catechumen, I once wrote, "I cannot receive Communion until I am chrismated, and I long for that day with a deep yearning in my heart." Receiving Holy Communion with a pure and humble heart in a spirit of love for God and neighbor may be the best place to begin to attain union and communion with our infinite and uncreated God.

The fruit and result of Christ's death and resurrection is *koinonia*: the community, communion, and fellowship of the Church.[408] This profound participation with God and with one another involves more than just social fellowship. *Koinonia* incorporates the saving call of Christ into our hearts to bring us into a new mode of existence as we richly share our lives with both Christ and other believers.[409] As Jesus eats and drinks with sinners, God offers the gift of eternal life to all of us in Christ.[410]

---

[407] John 6:56 KJV.
[408] Kesich, *The Birth of the Church: AD 33-200*, 33.
[409] Kodell, *The Eucharist in the New Testament*, 73.
[410] Ibid., 107.

The Joy of Orthodoxy offers a simple way to focus each day on living a virtuous life. With seven virtues for the seven days of the week, you can begin and end each day with your heart and mind set upon a particular virtue. By taking some time to meditate on these realities during the day, you remind yourself of the importance of living a virtuous life. Here again are the seven daily virtues:

Monday: HUMILITY
Tuesday: PURITY
Wednesday: HOLINESS
Thursday: LOVE
Friday: LONGSUFFERING
Saturday: PRAYER
Sunday: JOY

There has been much joy in the journey of my conversion into Orthodoxy. "And the Church is love, expectation and joy. It is heaven on earth, according to our Orthodox tradition; it is the joy of recovered childhood, that free, unconditioned and disinterested joy which alone is capable of transforming the world."[411] The source of this joy in my life is the experience of God Himself: "Having uncovered, O Saviour, a little of the light of Thy divinity to those who went up with Thee into the mountain, Thou hast made them lovers of Thy heavenly glory."[412] The Paschal Mystery continues to call me day by day, minute by minute, from

---

[411] Schmemann, *For the Life of the World*, 30.
[412] *The Festal Menaion*, 481.

death to life: "Thou hast taken me captive with longing for Thee, O Christ, and hast transformed me with Thy divine love. Burn up my sins with the fire of the Spirit, and count me worthy to take my fill of delight in Thee, that dancing with joy I may magnify both Thy Comings, O Lord who are good."[413]

"And now here is my secret, a very simple secret: It is only with the heart that one can see rightly; what is essential is invisible to the eye."[414] With the humility of a child and the wonder of a poet, I feel such a deep and abiding joy in my life like never before. I am home, finally home, and through the sacramental life of the Orthodox Church, I meet the Incarnate God every minute of every day. Still a victim of my immense pride, the temptation of lust, and an inherent selfishness, there is a deep and abiding love for my best friends Jesus and Mary, and I continue to experience great joy within my Orthodox journey.

The strategy outlined in this book is one of the simplest ways to begin to "pray without ceasing"[415] and experience the fullness of Orthodox Joy with grateful hearts centered completely on Christ. Strive in this simple way to embrace The Joy of Orthodoxy every minute of every day.

---

[413] Ibid., 494.
[414] Saint-Exupéry, *The Little Prince*, 73.
[415] 1 Thessalonians 5:17 NASB.

BIBLIOGRAPHY

Allen, Joseph J. ed. *And He Leads Them*. Ben Lomond, CA: Conciliar Press, 2001.

_____. *Inner Way*. Brookline, MA: Holy Cross Orthodox Press, 2000.

_____. *The Ministry of the Church: The Image of Pastoral Care*. Crestwood, NY: St. Vladimir's Seminary Press, 1986.

_____ ed. *Orthodox Synthesis: The Unity of Theological Thought*. Crestwood, NY: St. Vladimir's Seminary Press, 1981.

Athanasius, Saint. *The Life of Antony and the Letter to Marcellinus*. Translated by Robert Gregg. Mahwah, NJ: Paulist Press, 1980.

_____. *On the Incarnation*. Crestwood, NY: St. Vladimir's Seminary Press, 1996.

Atty, Alexander. "The Prodigal Son." Vespers. Saint Raphael of Brooklyn Orthodox Church, Chantilly, VA. 24 March 2012. Lecture.

Basil, Saint. *On the Holy Spirit*. Translated by Stephen Hildebrand. Yonkers, NY: St. Vladimir's Seminary Press, 2011.

Beeley, Christopher A. *Gregory of Nazianzus on the Trinity and the Knowledge of God*. New York: Oxford University Press, 2008.

Bloom, Metropolitan Anthony. *Beginning to Pray*. New York: Paulist Press, 1982.

Bobrinskoy, Boris. *The Mystery of the Trinity*. Crestwood, NY: St. Vladimir's Seminary Press, 1999.

Breck, John. *The Sacred Gift of Life*. Crestwood, NY: St. Vladimir's Seminary Press, 1998.

Cabasilas, Nicholas. *The Life in Christ*. Translated by Carmino J. deCatanzaro. Crestwood, NY: St. Vladimir's Seminary Press, 1974.

Cardine, Patrick. "Benediction-Adoration: A Beautiful Vision." The Orthodox West. https://www.orthodoxwest.com/beautiful-vision (accessed May 2, 2018).

Carlton, Clark. *The Life: The Orthodox Doctrine of Salvation*. Salisbury, MA: Regina Orthodox Press, 2000.

The Coptic Liturgy of St. Basil. Cairo, Egypt: St. John the Beloved Publishing House, 1993.

The Divine and Holy Liturgy of the Orthodox Church. Louisville, KY: St. Michael the Archangel Orthodox Church, 2007.

Donohue, Brian. Email to David Lochbihler. 23 December 2021.

Dostoevsky, Fyodor. *The Brothers Karamazov.* Translated by Constance Garnett, in *Great Books of the Western World*, vol. 52. Chicago: Encyclopaedia Britannica, 1952.

Eichaninov, Alexander. *The Diary of a Russian Priest.* Crestwood, NY: St. Vladimir's Seminary Press, 1967.

The Festal Menaion. Translated by Mother Mary and Kallistos Ware. South Canaan, PA: St. Tikhon's Seminary Press, 1969.

Hierotheos, Metropolitan of Nafpaktos. *Hesychia and Theology: The Context for Man's Healing in the Orthodox Church.* Translated by Sister Pelagia Selfe. Levadia, Greece: Birth of the Theotokos Monastery, 2007.

_____. *The Illness and Cure of the Soul in the Orthodox Theology*, 2nd ed. rev. Translated by Effie Mavromichali. Levadia, Greece: Birth of the Theotokos Monastery, 2010.

_____. *Orthodox Spirituality*, 5th ed. Translated by Effie Mavromichali. Levadia, Greece: Birth of the Theotokos Monastery, 2008.

Hildebrand, Stephen M. Introduction. *On the Holy Spirit*, by Saint Basil. Translated by Stephen Hildebrand. Yonkers, NY: St. Vladimir's Seminary Press, 2011, pp.11-26.

Hopkins, Gerard Manley. "God's Grandeur." *Poems of Gerard Manley Hopkins*, ed. W. H. Gardner. New York: Oxford University Press, 1948.

Kelly, J.N.D. *Early Christian Doctrines*, rev. ed. New York: HarperOne, 1978.

Kennedy, Robert F. "Excerpts from Remarks." Concordia Senior College, Fort Wayne, Indiana. 23 April 1968.

Kesich, Veselin. *The Birth of the Church: AD 33-200*, in The Church in History, vol. 1, part 1, *Formation and Struggles*. Crestwood, NY: St. Vladimir's Seminary Press, 2007.

Kodell, Jerome. *The Eucharist in the New Testament*. Collegeville, MN: Liturgical Press, 1991.

"Local Guardsmen at Riot Scene: Berwyn Outfits Relieve 44th Division Units; All Quiet in Disorder Area." *The Berwyn Life*. July 18, 1951, p. 1.

Lossky, Vladimir. *In the Image and Likeness of God.* Crestwood, NY: St. Vladimir's Seminary Press, 1985.

_____. *The Mystical Theology of the Eastern Church.* Crestwood, NY: St. Vladimir's Seminary Press, 1976.

_____. *Orthodox Theology: An Introduction.* Translated by Ian and Ihita Kesarcodi-Watson. Crestwood, NY: St. Vladimir's Seminary Press, 1978.

_____. *The Vision of God.* Crestwood, NY: St. Vladimir's Seminary Press, 1963.

Mantzaridis, Georgios. *The Deification of Man.* Crestwood, NY: St. Vladimir's Seminary Press, 1984.

Markides, Kyriacos. *Gifts of the Desert.* New York: Doubleday, 2005.

Meyendorff, Paul. *The Anointing of the Sick.* Crestwood, NY: St. Vladimir's Seminary Press, 2009.

Meyendorff, John. *Byzantine Theology: Historical Trends and Doctrinal Themes.* Crestwood, NY: St. Vladimir's Seminary Press, 1980.

Nouwen, Henri J. M., Donald P. McNeill, and Douglas A. Morrison. *Compassion.* New York: Doubleday, 1982.

Saint-Exupéry, Antoine de. *The Little Prince*. San Diego: Harcourt Brace, 1971.

Saliba, Metropolitan Philip and Joseph Allen. *Meeting the Incarnate God*. Brookline, MA: Holy Cross Orthodox Press, 2008.

The Sayings of the Desert Fathers. Translated by Benedicta Ward. Kalamazoo, MI: Cistercian Publications, 1984.

Schmemann, Alexander. *The Eucharist*. Crestwood, NY: St. Vladimir's Seminary Press, 1987.

_____. *For the Life of the World*, 2nd ed. rev. Crestwood, NY: St. Vladimir's Seminary Press, 1973.

_____. *Great Lent*. Crestwood, NY: St. Vladimir's Seminary Press, 1969.

_____. *Introduction to Liturgical Theology*. Crestwood, NY: St. Vladimir's Seminary Press, 2003.

_____. *Of Water & the Spirit*. Crestwood, NY: St. Vladimir's Seminary Press, 1974.

Stavropouplos, Christoforos. *Partakers of Divine Nature*. Minneapolis, MN: Light and Life Publishing, 1976.

Walker, Williston, Richard Norris, David Lotz, and Robert Handy. *A History of the Christian Church*, 4th ed. New York: Scribner, 1985.

Ware, Kallistos. Letter to David Lochbihler. 28 July 2012.

_____. *The Orthodox Way*. Crestwood, NY: St. Vladimir's Seminary Press, 1979.

Ware, Timothy. *The Orthodox Church*. London: Penguin Books, 1997.

Wordsworth, William. " 'My Heart Leaps Up When I Behold.'" *Selected Poems of William Wordsworth*, ed. Solomon Francis Gingerich. Boston: Houghton Mifflin Company, 1923.

Zizioulas, John D. *Being as Communion*. Crestwood, NY: St. Vladimir's Seminary Press, 1985.

ABOUT THE AUTHOR

Deacon David Lochbihler, J.D., celebrated *The Joy of Orthodoxy* on the day of his Diaconate Ordination during the Feast of Saint Patrick in 2019 at Saint Patrick Orthodox Church in Virginia. He also teaches fourth grade at The Fairfax Christian School in Northern Virginia. After graduating *summa cum laude* from the University of Notre Dame and *cum laude* from the University of Texas School of Law, Deacon David worked as a Chicago attorney for three years before becoming a teacher and coach for three decades. He earned Master's degrees in Elementary Education, Biblical Studies, and Orthodox Theology. His varsity high school basketball and soccer teams captured four N.V.I.A.C. conference championships. Deacon David authored *Prayers to Our Lady East and West* in 2021.

PRAYERS
TO OUR LADY
EAST AND WEST

DEACON DAVID LOCHBIHLER, J.D.

ORTHODOX LOGOS PUBLISHING

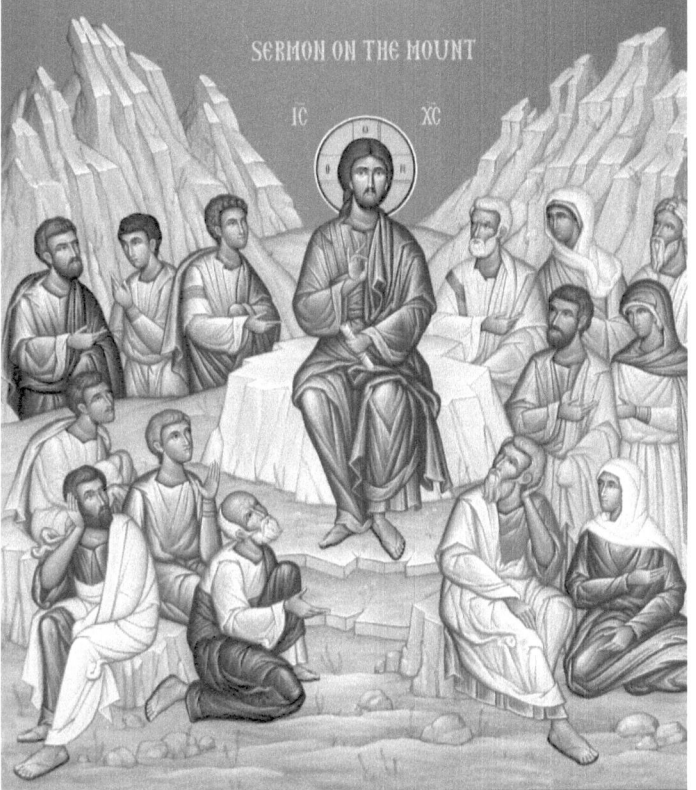

ORTHODOX LOGOS PUBLISHING

SERMON ON THE MOUNT

JAMES KENNETH HAMRICK

ORTHODOX PREACHING

AS THE ORAL ICON OF CHRIST

Dr. Charalambos M. Bousias

ELDER ANTHIMOS OF SAINT ANNE'S

The wise and God-bearing contemporary Father of Athos

www.ingramcontent.com/pod-product-compliance
Lightning Source LLC
Chambersburg PA
CBHW030303100526
44590CB00012B/501